JUDICIAL PUZZLES.

Gathered from the State Trials.

BY

JOHN PAGET, Esq.,

Barrister-at-law, Recorder of Thames Police Court.

SAN FRANCISCO:

Sumner Whitney & Co.

1876.

LEGAL RECREATIONS.

VOL. III.

Judicial Puzzles.

PREFACE.

These narratives and reviews of five most interesting State trials were published in "Blackwood's Magazine" in 1859–60, and subsequently reprinted, among other contributions of the same author, in a volume entitled "Paradoxes and Puzzles."

The publishers present this American edition with the belief that it will prove attractive to general readers as well as the legal profession and add a pleasant variety to the series of "LEGAL RECREATIONS."

January, 1876.

CONTENTS.

I. Elizabeth Canning.

II. The Campden Wonder.

Trial of the Perrys for Murder of Harrison.

III. The Annesley Case.

IV. Eliza Fenning.

V. Spencer Cowper's Case.

JUDICIAL PUZZLES.

I.

ELIZABETH CANNING.

Every one has heard of the case of Elizabeth Canning. It is constantly quoted, constantly relied upon as an authority for propositions the most diverse and even contradictory. There is a general vague idea that an ingenious fraud was by some marvelous agency detected, that innocence was rescued from imminent peril, and truth vindicated; but by what means or under what circumstances this took place, who was innocent and who was guilty, very few of those in whose mouths the name of the case is most familiar would be able to say. To any one who has taken the pains to make himself master of the case, this hazy condition of mind will be anything but surprising. It is, in truth, perhaps, the most complete and most inexplicable Judicial Puzzle on record; and after reading four hundred and twenty-nine pages of close bad print, in the 19th volume of the "State Trials," a candid man will find himself equally amazed at the zeal, the industry, the ingenuity with which it was sought to discover where the truth really lay; and the way in which, notwithstanding the fullest and most patient inquiry, that truth, though apparently close at hand, still eluded its pursuers.

Elizabeth Canning was a servant girl in the family of a man of the name of Edward Lyon, a carpenter in Aldermanbury. At the time in question (1753) she was about eighteen years of age. Her father had, during his lifetime, been also in the employment of Mr. Lyon; her mother resided in the immediate neighborhood. She had previously been in the service of another neighbor of the name of Wintlebury for nearly two years: there was every opportunity and every motive for the strictest examination of her character, and it bore the investigation without the slightest stain being detected. On the 1st of January, 1753, her mistress gave Elizabeth Canning permission to spend the day with an uncle of the name of Colley, who lived at Saltpetre Bank, now known as Dock Street, near Well-Close Square, and immediately behind the London Dock. In the evening Colley and his wife accompanied her on her way back to her master's in Aldermanbury as far as Houndsditch, where they parted from her soon after nine o'clock. At this point she was lost sight of. She did not return to her master's nor to her mother. The surprise, alarm, and anxiety of her friends were extreme. Advertisements were repeatedly inserted in the papers, offering rewards for her discovery. It was said that a shriek had been heard, as of some female in distress, in a hackney-coach in Bishopsgate Street, and attempts were made to find the driver, but in vain. No trace of the lost girl could be discovered.

On the 29th of January, about a quarter after ten o'clock in the evening, just as they were preparing to fasten up the house, and to go to bed, the latch of her mother's door was lifted, and a figure entered, pale, tottering, emaciated, livid, bent almost double, with no clothes but her shift, a wretched petticoat, and a filthy bed-gown, a rag tied over her head, bloody from a wound on her ear. Such was the condition in which Elizabeth Canning returned after an absence of four weeks. Where had she been? what had happened to her during those weeks?

The first question which presents itself is, What was the account given by the girl herself? Then follows the inquiry how far that account is supported, or in what respects is it contradicted, by evidence subsequently produced? As we proceed, we shall find ourselves involved in a most perplexing and difficult investigation, but for the present we may confine our attention to Canning's own account. It was given in the presence of many witnesses, without apparent preparation or concert with any one—indeed there was no time for this, as, immediately upon her arrival, the neighbors flocked in to express their sympathy and satisfy their curiosity. Few minutes had elapsed before the house was full.

Her former master, Mr. Wintlebury, (who seems to have had a very kindly feeling towards her, and who gave her the highest character) was among them; another neighbor, of the name of Robert Scarratt, was also there, and many more. The statement made by Canning in reply to their inquiries was, that as she passed through Moorfields, after parting from her uncle and aunt, she was attacked by two men, who robbed her of what money she had about her, stripped off her gown, and struck her a blow which rendered her insensible. That when she came to herself, she found that she was being dragged along a road; that about four o'clock in the morning they arrived at a house, into which she was carried by these two men; "when she came in, there was an elderly woman and two young ones; the old woman took hold of her arm and asked if she would go their way? and she said No. Then she went and took a knife out of a drawer, and cut the lacing of her stays and took them off, and gave her a great slap in the face, and told her she should suffer in the flesh, and opened a door, and shoved her up a pair of stairs into a room."* This room she described as a "longish, darkish room,"† in which there was some hay,‡ a pitcher of water, some pieces of bread—about as much as would be equal in quantity to a quartern loaf; that there was a fireplace and a grate, out of which she took the bedgown she had on, and the rag which was tied over her head; that there was a cask, a saddle, a pewter basin, and a few other articles, which she specified, in the room; that the house was ten or eleven miles from London on the Hertfordshire road; that there was a staircase near the room, up and down which she heard persons pass-

* Evidence of Mary Myers, 19 State Trials, 504.
† Scarratt, 496-501.
‡ Myers, 505.

ing during the night; and that she had heard "the name of Mother Wills or Mother Wells mentioned." Whether this last statement as to the name of Wells was made in reply to a suggestion or not, is, however, doubtful—Scarratt stating that it was in reply to an expression used by him when he heard she had been on the Hertfordshire road, that he would "lay a guinea to a farthing she had been at Mother Wells's";* whilst Mary Myers states that Canning had mentioned the name of Wells to her before Scarratt spoke, and that if Scarratt had spoken previously she must have heard him.† She certainly said she had been confined in a room on the Hertfordshire road before any suggestion had been made to her;‡ and when asked "how she knew that?" accounted for it by saying that she had seen, through the crevices of the boards which were nailed over the window, a coachman, to whom she had been accustomed to carry parcels for her master addressed to Hertford, and by whose coach her mistress had been in the habit of traveling, drive past the house. She said, that after remaining confined in this room, with no other food than the bread and water, and a minced pie which she happened to have in her pocket, from the 1st of January till the 29th, she escaped out at the window by pulling some of the boards down, and in doing so tore her ear.§ She described the woman who robbed her of her stays as a "tall, black, swar-

* Scarratt, 495.

† Myers, 505; Wintlebury, 510.

‡ Woodward, 507; Wintlebury, 510.

§ Myers, 505.

thy woman."* Scarratt, whose suspicions had, as we have seen, pointed at Wells, immediately observed that "that description did not answer to her."† She then described very particularly the course she took through the fields, past a tan-yard and over a little bridge into the high-road, after making her escape through the window. This description was, however, given in reply to leading questions put by Scarratt; but it is worthy of remark that she said she met a man, and asked her road to London‡—a fact which, as we shall presently see, was subsequently confirmed by the evidence of a witness of the name of Bennett.§

Such in substance was the account given by Elizabeth Canning on the evening of the 29th of January. Is it a matter of surprise that such a story, told by a young girl at the moment of her restoration to her family, spoken in the starts and snatches of extreme debility and exhaustion, attested by her emaciated form, her pallid cheek, her numb and withered limbs, should find deep sympathy and ready relief from those who had known her from childhood, who had listened day by day, for four weeks, to the lamentations of her mother, and who had felt, as every day passed, their hopes grow fainter, and their fears assume more and more the aspect of certainty? And, after all, is there such improbability on the face of the story as should induce us even now to reject it as incredible? The robbery in Moorfields was the

* Woodward, 508; Scarratt, 496.

† Scarratt, 496.

‡ Scarratt, 496.

§ Bennett, 527.

most probable of occurrences. It is impossible to take up a newspaper of that period without finding similar outrages recorded. It is true that it is difficult to assign any motive that could induce the robbers to encumber themselves with the strongest proof of their crime, by carrying her off; but it is equally difficult to suggest any cause other than that which she herself assigned for the condition to which she was reduced. An attempt was made during the proceedings to show a connection to have existed between Elizabeth Canning and the witness Scarratt, but the attempt utterly failed. Scarratt swore (and he would have been easily contradicted had he sworn falsely) that he had no acquaintance with the girl; and although he resided in the neighborhood, he believed he had never even seen her until the night of her return to her mother's house. It was upon her saying that she had been on the Hertfordshire road that his suspicions pointed to Wells' house, which he had before known as one of evil repute, as the place of her confinement; but his good faith is shown by his admission that he mentioned the name of Wells to her first, and the description which Canning gave of the room could not have been suggested by his questions, as he had never been in it.* The description which she gave of the woman who cut off her stays is also conclusive that she was not prompted by Scarratt, who, when he heard it, immediately said that it did not answer to Wells, who was the person he suspected.

* Scarratt, 498.

On the day but one after, the 31st of January, Canning repeated her story to Alderman Chitty, who was the sitting alderman at the time, and who thereupon issued his warrant for the apprehension of Mother Wells.

On the 1st of February, Canning, accompanied by her mother and her friends, went with the officer who had charge of the warrant to Enfield Wash.

The house of Mother Wells still stands a little beyond the tenth milestone on the Hertford road. It is on the right hand, at the corner of the lane leading down to the Ordnance Factory Station of the Eastern Counties Railway. The shell has been but little altered, and the rooms still remain nearly the same as they appear on the plan which was published in the "Gentleman's Magazine" for 1753. If the truth of Elizabeth Canning's story was to be proved in the same way as Jack Cade's royal descent, "the bricks are alive to this day to testify it." The window through which she escaped still commands a view of the road to Hertford. Chingford Hill might still, but for the cottages which have sprung up in consequence of the railway station, be seen, as she described, from the other window. The pantiles of the roof still remain unpointed, and everything bears testimony to the truth of her description. But instead of Mother Wells and her gang of tramps and gipsies, we found, on our visit to Enfield Wash, a comely matron presiding at a table surrounded by bonny lasses and chubby boys from sixteen downwards, whose laughing blue eyes and clear, rosy complexions formed as strong and agreeable a contrast to poor Elizabeth Canning as the bright furniture, cheerful hearth, and blazing fire did to the desolation, filth, and discomfort which formerly prevailed in that now comfortable dwelling. Assuredly fate seems to have mingled a very fair allowance of sugar and nutmeg in the cup of Mr. Negus—for such is the jolly name of the present occupant of the house, who seems to be, and we trust is, driving a prosperous trade as a baker.

Canning was carried from room to room, and at last into the loft. She immediately said, "This is the room I was in, but there is more hay in it than there was when I was here;"* and she pushed some of the hay aside with her foot, and showed two holes in the floor which she had observed. She pointed out the cask, the saddle, the pitcher, the tobacco-mould, and the pewter basin,† which she had mentioned on her arrival at her mother's; and she correctly described the view which might be seen from each of the windows. On examination, the boards which closed up the window at which she said she had escaped, were found to have been only fastened there very recently, as "the wood was fresh split with driving a great nail through it, and the crack seemed as fresh as could be."‡

Could there be stronger confirmation of the truth of her story? By what means could Canning have acquired this accurate knowledge? It has been said that the room did not agree with Canning's

* Myers, 506.
† Scarratt, 497 : Myers, 506.
‡ Adamson, 517.

description. A careful examination of the evidence shows, however, that it coincided with that description in the most remarkable manner. There were, no doubt, some discrepancies—for instance, Canning had mentioned a *grate*, and there proved to be none. She had spoken of *a* saddle, and *three* were found. She had spoken of being *locked* in, whilst in fact the door was fastened only with a button or bolt. There were some other trifling inaccuracies.

Suspicion had pointed at Wells as the person who had committed the outrage; but when Canning was brought into the room in which all the inmates of the house were collected, contradicting the expectation of her friends, she passed Wells by unnoticed, and, pointing to an old gipsy woman of the name of Mary Squires, who was sitting by the fire, said, "That old woman in the corner was the woman that robbed me." The gipsy rose from her seat, drew aside the cloak in which she was partially muffled, and displayed a face such as, once seen, could not easily be forgotten. She was, as Canning had described her, "tall, dark, and swarthy." She looked steadfastly at Canning, and exclaimed, "Me rob you! I never saw you in my life before. For God Almighty's sake do not swear my life away! Pray, madam, look at this face; if you have once seen it before, you must have remembered it: for God Almighty, I think, never made such another. Pray, madam, when do you say I robbed you?" Canning said it was on the first day of the new year. "Lord bless me!" exclaimed the gipsy, "I was a hundred and twenty miles from this place then!" George Squires, the gipsy's son, immediately added, "We were in Dorsetshire at that time, at a place called Abbotsbury; we went there to keep our Christmas." Here we arrive at the beginning of what makes this case so remarkable. We have insisted on the importance of the first account given by Canning. The gipsy and her son are entitled to a like consideration. This prompt and ready *alibi*, asserted without hesitation, specifying time and place with undoubting accuracy, and thus affording means for testing its truth, gave occasion to the very remarkable conflict of testimony which followed, and which entitles this case to its rank as one of the most interesting on record. An *alibi* is, as has often been remarked, the best or the worst of defenses. It often depends upon a few miles or even a few yards of distance, or upon a clock being a few minutes fast or slow. No such nicety arises in this case. The robbery was committed early on the morning of the 1st of January—New Year's Day—a date easily fixed. Abbotsbury is a hundred and fifty miles, as the crow flies, from Enfield: the gipsy understated the distance. It also often involves difficult questions of personal identity. None such arise here. The gipsy spoke truly when she said that "God Almighty never made such another face as hers." She was not only singularly hideous, but deeply marked with the scars of disease; and the witnesses who were examined had many of them been long familiar with her appearance. These circumstances seem to exclude the possibility of mistake on the part of the witnesses. Must we then resort to the conclusion that one side or the other is guilty of perjury? This hypothesis, though easy and simple enough at first sight, will be found on investigation to be attended with nearly as many difficulties as any other. We must, however, go back to Elizabeth Canning, whom we left in Mother Wells' kitchen, confronted by the gipsy and her son. In the house, besides the gipsy and her family, was a man of the singular name of Fortune Natus and his wife, and a young woman named Virtue Hall. The whole party were forthwith taken to the residence of the nearest magistrate, Mr. Teshmaker, of Ford's Grove, by whom all were discharged with the exception of the gipsy and Mother Wells, who were committed to prison to take their trial, the one for stealing Canning's stays, and the other as accessory to the felony.

A new actor now comes on the stage, and a curious insight is afforded into the mode in which inquiries of this nature were conducted in the metropolis a hundred years ago.

Henry Fielding, the celebrated novelist, was then a police magistrate of London.

To tell a tale told by Fielding in any words but his own would indeed be presumption.

"Upon the 6th of February," he says,* "as I was sitting in my room, Counselor Maden being then with me, my clerk delivered me a case, which was thus, as I remember, indorsed at the top: 'The case

* A Clear State of the Case of Elizabeth Canning, by Henry Fielding, Esq., 1753, p. 30.

of Elizabeth Canning, for Mr. Fielding's opinion'; and at the bottom, 'Salt, Solr.' Upon the receipt of this case, with my fee, I bid my clerk give my service to Mr. Salt, and tell him that I would take the case with me into the country, whither I intended to go the next day, and desired he would call for it on the Friday morning afterwards; after which, without looking into it, I delivered it to my wife, who was then drinking tea with us, and who laid it by. The reader will pardon my being so particular in these circumstances, as they seem, however trifling they may be in themselves, to show the true nature of this whole transaction, which hath been so basely misrepresented, and as they will all be attested by a gentleman of fashion, and of as much honor as any in the nation. My clerk presently returned up-stairs, and brought Mr. Salt with him, who, when he came into the room, told me that he believed the question would be of little difficulty, and begged me earnestly to read it over then, and give him my opinion, as it was a matter of some haste, being of a criminal nature, and he feared the parties would make their escape. Upon this, I desired him to sit down; and when the tea was ended, I ordered my wife to fetch me back the case, which I then read over, and found it to contain a very full and clear state of the whole affair relating to the usage of this girl, with a query what methods might be proper to take to bring the offenders to justice; which query I answered in the best manner I was able. Mr. Salt then desired that Elizabeth Canning might swear to her information before me; and added that it was the very particular desire of several gentlemen of that end of the town, that Virtue Hall might be examined by me relating to her knowledge of this affair. This business I at first declined, partly as it was a transaction which had happened at a distant part of the country, as it had been examined already by a gentleman with whom I have the pleasure of some acquaintance, and of whose worth and integrity I have, with all, I believe, who know him, a very high opinion; but principally, indeed, for that I had been almost fatigued to death with several tedious examinations at that time, and had intended to refresh myself with a day or two's interval in the country, where I had not been, unless on a Sunday, for a long time. I yielded, however, at last, to the importunities of Mr. Salt; and my only motives for so doing were, besides those importunities, some curiosity, occasioned by the extraordinary nature of the case, and a great compassion for the dreadful condition of the girl, as it was represented to me by Mr. Salt.

"The next day Elizabeth Canning was brought in a chair to my house, and being led up-stairs between two, the following information, which I had never before seen, was read over to her, when she swore to the truth, and set her mark to it."

Here follows Canning's information, somewhat expanded from the one made before Alderman Chitty, but in the main the same.

"Upon this information," continues Fielding, "I issued a warrant against all who should be found resident in the house of the said Wells, as idle and disorderly persons, and persons of evil name, that they might appear before me, and give security for their good behavior; upon which warrant, Virtue Hall and one Judith Natus were seized and brought before me, both being found at Mother Wells'. They were in my house above an hour or more before I was at leisure to see them, during which time, and before I had ever seen Virtue Hall, I was informed that she would confess the whole matter. When she came before me she appeared in tears, and seemed all over in a trembling condition, upon which I endeavored to soothe and comfort her. The word I first spoke to her, as well as I can remember, were these: 'Child, you need not be under this fear and apprehension; if you will tell us the whole truth of this affair, I give you my word and honor, as far as it is in my power to protect you, you shall come to no manner of harm.' She answered that she would tell the whole truth, but desired to have some time given her to recover from her fright. Upon this, I ordered a chair to be brought her, and desired her to sit down; and then, after some minutes, began to examine her, which I continued doing in the softest language and kindest manner I was able, for a considerable time, till she had been guilty of so many prevarications and contradictions that I told her I would examine her no longer, but would commit her to prison, and leave her to stand or fall by the evidence against her; and at the same time advised Mr. Salt to prosecute her as a felon, together with the gipsy woman. Upon this she begged I would hear her once more, and said that she would tell the whole truth, and accounted for her unwillingness to do it from her fears of the gipsy woman and Wells. I then asked her a few questions, which she answered with more appearance of truth than she had done before; after which I recommended to Mr. Salt to go with her, and take her information in writing; and at her parting from me, I bid her to be a good girl, and be sure to say neither more nor less than the whole truth. During this whole time there were no less than ten or a dozen persons of credit present, who will, I suppose, testify the truth of this whole transaction as it is here related. Virtue Hall then went from me, and returned in about two hours; when the following information, which was, as she said, taken from her mouth, was read over to her, and signed with her mark."

The information of Virtue Hall, as might be expected from the circumstances under which it was taken, is a mere echo to that of Canning.

What should we think at the present day of a magistrate who received a fee and instructions from a prosecuting solicitor, who hesitated to investigate a charge of felony because he wanted a day or two of relaxation in the country, who alternately coaxed and threatened the prisoner who had been brought before him on his own warrant, until he had obtained a confession, and who then allowed that prisoner to be closeted in private with the attorney for the prosecution, and to be sworn to an information procured from her by the attorney during that interview, and produced ready cut and dried! The *naïveté* with which Fielding tells the story is amusing. He was clearly unconscious that he was doing anything wrong or even irregular, and no doubt such a proceeding was by no means unusual. But the evidence of Virtue Hall is under these circumstances utterly worthless. We need feel no surprise that she afterwards, when the pressure came from the other side, retracted every word she had sworn, and her testimony may be cast out of the case altogether.* We still get no further than the evidence of Elizabeth Canning herself.

On the 21st of February, 1753, Mary Squires and Susannah Wells were placed at the bar of the Old Bailey. Canning told her story; Virtue Hall corroborated it point by point. The condition in which she returned home, and the circumstances attending the capture of Squires and Wells, were proved as we have narrated them. Squires was then called upon for her defense. She said nothing, but called three witnesses. John Gibbons, who kept a public-house at Abbotsbury, near Dorchester, swore that Squires was at his house from the 1st of January to the 9th. William Clarke corroborated this statement. Thomas Greville, of Coombe, near Salisbury, deponed that she was at his house on the 14th of January. To meet this evidence, a man of the name of Iniser was called on behalf of the prosecution to prove that he had seen Squires in the neighborhood of Enfield about the time in question—namely, the first week in January. Wells, on being called upon, admitted that her character would not bear investi-

* State Trials, xix. 455, 275; Gascoyne's Report; Dr. Hill's pamphlet. See "A full and authentic Account," etc., p. 66.

gation. She was what was called in the slang of the day (rendered classic by Mr. Harrison Ainsworth and the Newgate-Calendar school of novelists) a "hempen widow." Her husband had been "unfortunate." It is curious to watch the changes of language. A word which then meant that a scoundrel had been hanged, now only implies that he has obtained a second-class certificate from a commissioner of bankruptcy. Both were convicted. On the last day of the session they were called up for sentence. Squires then said that she was at Greville's house at Coombe on New Year's Day, on the next day at Stopage, on the Thursday in New Year's week at Basingstoke, on Friday at Bagshot, on Saturday at Old Brentford, where she remained on Sunday and Monday; and that she came to Enfield on the Tuesday following. This account, being inconsistent with that given by Gibbons, who had sworn that from the 1st to the 9th of January she was at his house at Abbotsbury, was considered to be conclusive of the falsehood of her defense. It seems to have been overlooked that the gipsy reckoned by the old style, which reconciles the two statements within two days—no very serious discrepancy when made by an ignorant and illiterate woman. Squires was sentenced to death; Wells was condemned to be branded on the hand, and imprisoned for six months. The first part of this sentence was immediately executed; and as the poor wretch's hand hissed under the glowing iron, and she writhed and screamed in agony, a yell of delight burst from the brutal mob who crowded the session-house.

There was, however, happily one man present, of sense and humanity. Sir Crispe Gascoyne, who presided over the court by virtue of his office as Lord Mayor, doubted the correctness of the verdict. He instituted a close and careful inquiry. He found the evidence of the Abbotsbury men confirmed by their neighbors. Virtue Hall retracted her evidence.* These facts he laid before the Crown on making his report of the convicts. They were referred to the law-officers. Squires was respited. The Attorney and Solicitor-General reported that the weight of the evidence was in the convict's favor, and upon this she received a free pardon.

A war of pamphlets now commenced; as many as thirty-six were published. Fielding on the one side and Ramsay the painter on the other, became respectively the champions of Canning and the gipsy. The newspapers were filled with the controversy. Portraits of Canning and of the gipsy (the latter of which fully bear out the report of her ugliness) were displayed in the shop windows, together with plans and views of Wells' house, and terrific representations of the principal incidents of the story. Grub Street thrived. To its hungry inhabitants

> "Betty Canning was at least,
> With Gascoyne's help, a six months' feast."†

The town was divided into Egyptians and Canningites. Families were split up into factions. Old friends who took different sides quarreled. Mobs

*Report, State Trials, xix, 275.
† Churchill Ghost, 182.

paraded the streets, blockaded the entrances to the courts, and attacked Sir Crispe Gascoyne in his coach. Never, probably, has a case which involved no public question created so much interest and excitement.

This state of things continued for fourteen months. At length, on the 29th of April 1754, Canning was placed at the same bar at which Squires had formerly stood, to take her trial for willful and corrupt perjury. Her trial lasted several days. The attention of the prosecution was directed principally to two points: first, to prove the *alibi* of the gipsy; and, secondly, to contradict Canning's story by the evidence of persons who had been in the room during the time she professed to have been confined there.

In support of the first of these issues they called as many as thirty-six witnesses; and certainly, if numbers, positiveness, and particularity could prove an issue, this was proved. But when the evidence comes to be examined, much of it is open to grave suspicion. George Squires, the gipsy's son, gave the most minute account of where he and his mother and sister were, and what they did during the month of January. He traced their course day by day, and from place to place. But when he was asked with regard to the rest of his journey, which he stated began about Michaelmas, he was totally unable to answer. His sister, who was in court the whole time, and who had accompanied George and his mother in their travels, was never examined at all, nor was the gipsy herself placed in the witness-box. It was obvious that the counsel for the prosecution feared that they would give inconsistent or contradictory accounts.

Upon the second issue, the principal witnesses were Fortune Natus and his wife, who swore that they slept in the loft every night during the month of January. If this was true, of course there is an end of the question. But it must be remembered that, long before they were examined, Virtue Hall had sworn that the hay in which they had slept in the kitchen was removed into the loft, and that they slept there after Canning's escape, on purpose to give color to this very story. It may also be asked, why was not this tale told on the trial of Squires? If true, the very first thing that would have been said, when Canning stated that she had been confined in that room, would have been, "That cannot be, for Natus and his wife slept there the whole of the time." Yet Natus and his wife were present when Canning was first brought down to Enfield; they were taken before Justice Teshmaker; they were present during the trial of Squires, when they were *not* examined, and this fact, conclusive, if true, is never heard of until fourteen months afterwards! Is it possible to place any reliance upon evidence given under such circumstances?

The argument most strongly relied upon as invalidating Canning's story, arises from the absence of motive on the part of any one to carry her off and shut her up as she described. Canning swore that she understood the gipsy's question, whether she "would go their way," to imply that she should lead a life of prostitution. This was the interpretation popularly adopted; and much of the sympathy which Canning obtained was given on the supposition that she was a girl whose virtue had been proof against both temptation and terror. But this hypothesis will not bear a moment's investigation. There is not one particle of evidence that she was exposed to any solicitations whatever of this kind. Nor, though it was the resort of tramps, gipsies, and other disreputable characters, does it appear that Mother Wells' was what is commonly understood by a house of ill-fame. But does the absence of assignable motive justify us in rejecting the story as untrue? Those who are familiar with criminal courts know well how slight and insignificant are the motives which often impel men to the most terrible crimes. Gleeson Wilson entered the house of Mrs. Henrickson, at Liverpool, apparently with no other intention but that of pilfering such small articles as he might have an opportunity of purloining as a lodger; but before he left it the next morning, he had committed four of the most atrocious murders on record. It is not more than three or four years since two boys, returning home from their work, in broad daylight, in the middle of London, were met by an apparently respectable man driving a Whitechapel cart, who inquired his way to some place in the neighborhood. One of the boys began to give him directions, when he asked the little fellow to get into the cart, and show him the road. Rejoicing in the certainty of a ride, and the hope of a sixpence, the poor boy got into the cart, and his companion went home to tea. He was never again seen alive. About six weeks afterwards, his body, naked, in a state of the most extreme emaciation, was found in a ditch near Acton. There was no external violence. *He had been starved to death.* The police exhausted every means that ingenuity could suggest, but in vain. No traces have ever been discovered how, why, or by whom this appalling crime was committed; nor has any motive for its commission been, so far as we are aware, even suggested. Had Elizabeth Canning died in the house of Mother Wells, and her body been thrown into a ditch in Enfield marsh, an equally impenetrable mystery would probably have shrouded her fate.

Highly improbable every one must admit Canning's story to be, and we must therefore look with the most critical caution upon the confirmatory evidence, before we permit ourselves to admit its truth. That confirmatory evidence divides itself into two classes. The first we may call the circumstantial confirmation, derived from its coincidence with existing facts. Such is the coincidence between her description of the room and its contents given on the 29th of January, with the condition of the room actually found on the first of February. Such, too, is the coincidence of the description previously given by Canning of the appearance of the woman who cut off her stays with the gipsy. This confirmation is of course weaker or stronger in proportion as it is tainted by or free from previous suggestions from other persons. Thus, her description of the room, which was independent of, and her description of the gipsy, which was contradictory to, Scarratt's suggestions, are worthy of much consideration; whilst her description of the fields through which she passed, of the tan-yard and the bridge, given in reply to his suggestive questions, is of little or no value. This we have already considered. The second class is the extrinsic confirmation derived from the testimony of witnesses, and this is again divided into that which supports Canning's story, and that which contradicts the *alibi* set up by Squires.

As to the first of these subdivisions, the evidence is scanty, but valuable as far as it goes. The keeper of the turnpike gate on Stamford Hill, about three miles from Moorfields, deposed that, one evening early in January, between ten and eleven o'clock, he heard "something of a sobbing crying voice" coming towards the gate from the direction of London. The night was still and dark, but as the noise approached he saw two men dragging a young woman along. They lifted her over the stile by the gate, and one of the men laughed and said with an oath, "How drunk she is!" Supposing this to be the case, and that the woman was the wife or sister of one of the men, besides considering that he was single-handed, he did not interfere, and they passed on in the direction of Enfield. He did not profess to identify Canning, nor to fix the time with any greater certainty than that it was the beginning of January.

It will be remembered that, on her arrival at home, Canning said, that soon after escaping from

Mother Wells', she asked her road to London. Thomas Bennett deponed, that on the afternoon of the 29th of January he met a girl in the most wretched and pitiable condition, and whose description exactly answered to Canning, about a quarter of a mile on the London side of Mother Wells' house; that she asked him the way to London, and he directed her. He fixed the date by other circumstances, and said that when, a day or two afterwards, he heard of Canning's escape, he exclaimed, "I'll be hanged if I did not meet the young woman near this place, and told her the way to London."

Daniel Dyer and Mary Cobb gave similar evidence as to having met a miserable looking girl about the same time and place, and the former spoke with some confidence to Canning as being that girl. It will be observed that the other witnesses merely speak to general similarity. But this, though at first sight it appears to detract from the value of their testimony, in fact adds to its weight. Had they not been giving truthful evidence, they would have made little scruple in swearing positively to Canning as being the person they saw.

Is it, then, likely that another girl, so closely answering the description both as to person and circumstances, (both being so remarkable) should have been dragged by two men along that road towards Enfield, at the same hour of the night, at the beginning of January, and have returned on the afternoon of the 29th? Such a coincidence appears almost beyond the bounds of possibility.

Here the evidence with regard to Canning ends.

To meet the *alibi* proved by the thirty-six Abbotsbury witnesses, twenty-six Enfield witnesses were called, who swore that they had seen Mary Squires at Enfield and in the neighborhood at various times during the latter end of December and beginning of January. They swore to the identity of Squires, whom many of them had long known, with the utmost certainty; they gave their reasons, some good and some bad, for remembering the time with the greatest accuracy. Their testimony seems to be in all respects equal, and in some superior, to that of the witnesses who had proved the *alibi*.

Here, then, we find the extraordinary fact of thirty-six witnesses positively swearing that a particular person, whom they well knew, was in Dorsetshire at a certain time, and twenty-six other witnesses swearing that the same person, whom they knew equally well, was at the same time a hundred and fifty miles off, in Middlesex! What are we to make of this? We have turned it over and over, looked at it this way and that way, read it backwards, and forwards, and upside down, and there it remains, puzzling us like a horrid incubus or incomprehensible nightmare. Is any faith to be placed in human testimony? Read the evidence on one side, and it is impossible to refuse our assent to it. Read that on the other, and it is equally conclusive. The *alibi* and the *ibi* are each supported by a train of evidence which appears irresistible.

The Recorder told the jury that if they believed the Enfield witnesses, the Abbotsbury witnesses must be willfully perjured; but he forgot to add, that if they believed the Abbotsbury witnesses, an equally unpleasant consequence followed as to the Enfield witnesses.

The verdict of the jury was of a piece with the rest of the case. They found that Canning was "guilty of perjury, but *not willful and corrupt*."

This verdict was of course an acquittal, but the Recorder refused to receive it; whereupon the jury "turned their backs upon themselves," and having first declared on their oaths that she was *not* guilty of willful and corrupt perjury, declared on the same oaths that she *was*. And to complete the mass of absurdity and contradiction, some of the jury afterwards made an affidavit that they believed Canning's story in the main, but found her guilty because they thought there was some discrepancy as to the day on which she had exhausted her pitcher of water.

Of the court, which, as then constituted, consisted of a mixed body of judges and city magistrates, nine members were for condemning the prisoner to transportation for seven years, and eight for inflicting only a short period of imprisonment, so evenly were opinions divided. She was accordingly transported. The sympathy and compassion which had been excited by her case did not cease. A considerable sum of money was collected for her. After the termination of her sentence she returned to England, and the last notice we find of her is the following, which is contained in the "Annual Register" for 1761, p. 179: "Elizabeth Canning is arrived in

England, and received a legacy of £500, left her three years ago by an old lady of Newington Green." Wells returned to Enfield, where she died, as appears by the parish register, on the 5th of October, 1763. What became of the gipsy we know not. Thus ends the case of Elizabeth Canning—a case eminently fitted to give occasion to the warmest, most eager, and most confident partisanship, inasmuch as it is almost impossible, after the coolest and most deliberate examination, to say to which side the balance of evidence inclines.

II.

The Campden Wonder.

The little market-town of Chipping-Campden lies on the verge of the Cotswold Hills. It is a quaint old place, formed of one straggling street of low-gabled houses, with an ancient market-house in the middle. The ruins of Campden House, built in the year 1612 by Sir Baptist Hickes, (the princely merchant who erected Hickes' Hall, and gave it to the county of Middlesex) remain a monument of the loyalty of his grandson, Baptist Lord Noel, who burnt his magnificent mansion to prevent it from falling into the hands of the Parliament troops.

Railroads have only lately traversed this out-of-the-way part of England. It is not on the high-road to anywhere, and though the country around possesses beauties peculiarly its own, it has never been frequented by tourists. It is best known by the love which Shakespeare evidently bore to it. There can be no doubt that it was the haunt of his boyhood. When Slender taunts Master Page by telling him that he hears his "fallow greyhound was outrun on Cotswold," we may be sure that many a course on those wide and then open downs must have risen to Shakespeare's recollection. It is here, too, that he places that pleasant arbor in Justice Shallow's orchard, where he ate "a last year's pippen of his own graffing, with a dish of carraways, and so forth," with Falstaff and his "cousin Silence." It was "a goodly dwelling and a rich." Cousin Silence was, we have no doubt, a Campden man, and trolled out his fragments of carols at the little bowling-green there. Shakespeare tells us that he was a townsman. "Is old Double *of your town* living yet?" Old Double, who is immortal because he died. "See, see!—he drew a good bow. And dead!—he shot a fine shoot. John of Gaunt loved him well, and betted much money on his head. Dead! How a score of good ewes now? And is old Double dead?"

He probably acquired the skill as an archer, which endeared him to "John of Gaunt," at those games on Dover's Hill, in the immediate neighborhood, which were celebrated by Ben Jonson, and which were held there annually until a few years ago. "Will Squele," too, was a "Cotswold man." Shakespeare must have loved the place, or he never would have coined so endearing a name. Who has not a kindly feeling towards Will Squele? The commentators have puzzled themselves greatly after their usual fashion, and have devised ingenious and improbable reasons why Falstaff's tailor should be one "Master Dombledon." They have sought for abstruse meanings in the name, stupidly fancying that it was originally written Doubledone, and implied a double charge. It is simply the name of a hill a few miles beyond Campden, and the use of it affords an additional proof of Shakespeare's familiarity with the country.

This little town was, in the year 1660, the scene of a tragedy so extraordinary that it is still remembered by the name of "The Campden Wonder."

On the 16th of August in that year, an old man of the name of William Harrison, who was steward to Lady Campden, and resided in the part of Campden House which still remained habitable, went on foot to Charringworth, a village about two miles distant, to receive some rents. He did not return so soon as was expected, and his wife, feeling some alarm at his absence, sent his servant, John Perry, to meet him, about eight or nine o'clock. Neither Perry nor his master returning that night, the son of the latter set out early in the morning in search of his father. On his way towards Charringworth he met Perry, who told him that his father was not at that place, and they went together in search of him to Ebrington, (a village between Campden and Charringworth) where they were informed that Harrison had called the evening before at the house of a man of the name of Daniel, on his return from Charringworth, but had almost immediately proceeded on his way towards Campden. This was the last they could hear of the old man. But in the meantime a hat and comb, much hacked and cut, and a band stained with blood, which was recognized as having been worn by him on that night, were found in a wild spot, near a large furze brake, between Ebrington and Campden. The report immediately, and very naturally, arose that Mr. Harrison had been waylaid, robbed, and murdered, and the whole population of the town turned out to search for his body. Their search was in vain—no trace of it could be discovered. Suspicion fell upon John Perry. The spot where the hat was found was just where he would have been likely to have met him on his return. He knew that he was going to receive a considerable sum of money. His master had left Ebrington safe. Perry's absence during the whole of the night was suspicious. The natural thing would have been, had he failed to meet his master, to have returned at once to Campden. He was taken into custody, and the next day was brought before a justice of peace. The account he gave was, that he had started on his way towards Charringworth immediately upon receiving his mistress' orders to do so; that after going a short distance, he met a man of the name of Reed, and, feeling afraid to go on in the dark, had returned with him to Campden; that he had started again with one Pearce, and, after going a short distance, had again returned. That he then went into the hen-roost, where he remained till about twelve o'clock, when, the moon having risen, he took courage and again set out; but a mist rising, he lost his way, and lay under a hedge till morning, when he went on to Charringworth, and inquired for his master of one Edward Plaisterer, who told him that he had paid him twenty-three pounds the afternoon previous. That he made further inquiries, but without success; and on his return home, about five o'clock in the morning, met his master's son. This account, which was confirmed by the three men he referred to, was not considered satisfactory, and, after remaining in custody about a week, Perry expressed a desire to be taken before the justice, to whom he said he would disclose what he would discover to no one else.

He then said that, ever since he had been in his master's service, his mother and his brother had been urging him to join them in robbing him. That their scheme was to waylay him on his return from receiving the rents. That he had accordingly informed his brother, on the morning of the day when Mr. Harrison went to Charringworth, of the errand upon which he had gone. That on the same evening, immediately after he had received his mistress' orders, he met his brother, and they went together towards Charringworth. That he watched his master, on his return, go into a field called the Conygree, through which a private path, which he was in the habit of using, led to his house. That he told his brother that "if he followed him he might have his money, and he in the meantime would walk a turn in the fields." That soon afterwards, following his brother, he found his master on the ground in the middle of the field, his brother upon him, and his mother standing by. That his master was not then dead, for he exclaimed, "Ah, rogues! will you kill me?" That he begged his brother not to kill him; but he replied, "Peace, peace! you are a fool"—and strangled him. That his brother took a bag of money out of his master's pocket, and threw it into his mother's lap; that they then carried the body into the garden, intending to throw it into a large sink; that he left it in the garden, and went to watch and listen, whilst, as he believed, his mother and brother put the body into the sink; but whether they did so or not he could not positively say. That going back into the town he met Pearce, and went with him towards Charringworth, as he had before stated. That he then returned to the hen-roost, and taking his master's hat, band, and comb, he cut them with his knife, and threw them in the road where they were found.

Upon this, strict search was made for the body, not only in the place which Perry had mentioned, but in all ponds in the neighborhood, and amongst the ruins of Campden House—but in vain. Joan and Richard Perry, the mother and brother of John, were taken into custody. They vehemently protested their innocence, and upbraided John for his falsehood. He still, however, stuck to his story, and retorted upon them with bitter reproaches for having urged him to the commission of so horrible a crime—affirming that he had spoken nothing but the truth, and declaring that he was ready to justify it to his death.

Immediately after the examination of the prisoners before the magistrate, a very remarkable circumstance occurred. They were removed separately, and of course in custody, John being some distance in advance of Richard. The latter, "pulling a clout out of his pocket, dropped a ball of inkle, which one of his guard taking up, he desired him to restore, saying it was only his wife's hair-lace." The constable, finding a noose at the end of it, and feeling some suspicion, took it to John and asked him if he knew anything of it, on which John shook his head and said, "Yea, to his sorrow; for *that was the string his brother strangled his master with.*"

Unfortunately, the only narrative which exists of this singular case diverges at this point into matters irrelevant to the main issue; but at the spring assizes following, after an interval of something more than six months, the three Perrys were tried for the murder. Up to this time, John Perry had persisted in his story. On the trial, however, he, like his mother and brother, pleaded *not guilty*, and when his confession was proved, alleged that he was "then mad, and knew not what he said."

We are left in ignorance what evidence, beyond the confession of John, was produced at the trial. That there must have been some is clear, as that confession, though evidence against John, was none against his mother or Richard. All three were convicted, and a few days afterwards hanged, on Broadway Hill, within sight of the town of Campden.

As Joan Perry was suspected to be a witch, and was supposed to have bewitched her sons so as to prevent them from confessing, she was hanged first. "After which, Richard, being upon the ladder, professed, as he had done all along, that he was wholly innocent of the fact for which he was then to die; and that he knew nothing of Mr. Harrison's death, nor what was become of him; and did with great earnestness beg and beseech his brother (for the satisfaction of the whole world and his own conscience) to declare what he knew concerning him; but he, with a dogged and surly carriage, told the people he was not obliged to confess to them; yet immediately before his death he said he knew nothing of his master's death, nor what was become of him, but they might hereafter possibly hear."

John Perry was hanged in chains upon a gibbet placed on the Broadway Hill.

Some years afterwards Mr. Harrison returned to Campden. The account he gave of the cause of his disappearance, and of his adventures during the period of his absence, in a letter to Sir Thomas Overbury of Bourton, (the nephew and heir of the unhappy victim of the infamous Countess of Somerset) is so curious that we give it entire.*

"Honored Sir: In obedience to your commands, I give you this true account of my being carried away beyond the seas, my continuance there, and return home. On a Thursday, in the afternoon, in the time of harvest, I went to Charringworth to demand rents, due to my Lady Campden; at which time the tenants were busy in the fields, and late ere they came home, which occasioned my stay there till the close of the evening. I expected a considerable sum, but received only three-and-twenty pounds, and no more. In my return home (in the narrow passage, amongst Ebrington furzes) there met me one horseman, and said, 'Art thou there?' and I, fearing that he would have rid over me, struck his horse over the nose; whereupon he struck at me with his sword several blows, and ran it into my side, while I (with my little cane) made my defense as well as I could. At last another came behind me, run me into the thigh, laid hold on the collar of my doublet, and drew

*14 State Trials, 1313—note to the case of Captain Green.

me to a hedge near the place; then came in another. They did not take my money, but mounted me behind one of them, drew my arms about his middle, and fastened my wrists together with something that had a spring-lock to it, as I conceived, by hearing it give a snap as they put it on; then they threw a great cloak over me, and conveyed me away. In the night they alighted at a hay-rick which stood near unto a stone pit by a wall-side, where they took away my money. About two hours before day (as I heard one of them tell the other he thought it to be then) they tumbled me into the stone pit. They stayed (as I thought) about an hour at the hay-rick, when they took horse again. One of them bade me come out of the pit; I answered they had my money already, and asked what they would do with me; whereupon he struck me again, drew me out, and put a great quantity of money into my pockets, and mounted me again after the same manner; and on the Friday, about sunsetting, they brought me to a lone house upon a heath (by a thicket of bushes) where they took me down almost dead, being sorely bruised with the carriage of the money. When the woman of the house saw that I could neither stand nor speak, she asked them whether or no they had brought a dead man? They answered no, but a friend that was hurt, and they were carrying him to a chirurgeon. She answered, if they did not make haste, their friend would be dead before they could bring him to one. Then they laid me on cushions, and suffered none to come into the room but a little girl. There we stayed all night, they giving me some broth and strong waters; and in the morning, very early, they mounted me as before, and on Saturday night they brought me to a place where were two or three houses, in one of which I lay all night on cushions by their bedside. On Sunday morning they carried me from thence, and about three or four o'clock they brought me to a place by the sea-side, called Deal, where they laid me down on the ground; and one of them staying by me, the other two walked a little off to meet a man, with whom they talked, and in their discourse I heard them mention seven pounds; after which they went away together, and about half an hour after returned. The man (whose name, as I after heard, was Wrenshaw) said he feared I would die before he could get me on board. Then presently they put me into a boat, and carried me on shipboard, where my wounds were dressed. I remained in the ship (as near as I could reckon) about six weeks, in which time I was indifferently recovered of my wounds and weakness. Then the master of the ship came and told me (and the rest who were in the same condition) that he discovered three Turkish ships. We all offered to fight in the defense of the ship and ourselves, but he commanded us to keep close, and said he would deal with them well enough. A little while after he called us up, and when we came on the deck we saw two Turkish ships close by us; into one of them we were put, and placed in a dark hole, where how long we continued before we landed, I know not. When we were landed they led us two days' journey, and put us into a great house or prison, where we remained four days and a half; and then came to us eight men to view us, who seemed to be officers; they called us, and examined us of our trades and callings, which every one answered. One said he was a chirurgeon, another that he was a broadcloth weaver, and I (after two or three demands) said I had some skill in physic. We three were set by, and taken by three of those eight men that came to view us. It was my chance to be chosen by a grave physician of eighty-seven years of age, who lived near Smyrna, who had formerly been in England, and knew Crowland in Lincolnshire, which he preferred before all other places in England. He employed me to keep his still-house, and gave me a silver bowl, double gilt, to drink in. My business was most in that place; but once he set me to gather cotton wool, which I not doing to his mind, he struck me down to the ground, and after drew his stiletto to stab me; but I, holding up my hands to him, he gave a stamp, and turned from me, for which I render thanks to my Lord and Saviour Jesus Christ, who stayed his hand and preserved me. I was there about a year and three-quarters, and then my master fell sick on a Thursday, and sent for me, and calling me, as he used, by the name of Boll, told me he should die, and bade me shift for myself. He died on Saturday following, and I presently hastened with my bowl to a port almost a day's journey distant, the way to which place I knew, having been twice there, employed by my master about the carriage of his cotton wool. When I came thither, I addressed myself to two men who came out of a ship of Hamborough, which (as they said) was bound for Portugal within three or four days. I inquired of them for an English ship; they answered, there was none. I entreated them to take me into their ship; they answered, they durst not, for fear of being discovered by the searchers, which might occasion the forfeiture, not only of their goods, but also of their lives. I was very importunate with them, but could not prevail; they left me to wait on Providence, which at length brought another out of the same ship, to whom I made known my condition, craving his assistance for my transportation; he made me the like answer as the former, and was as stiff in his denial, till the sight of my bowl put him to a pause. He returned to the ship, and after half an hour's space he came back again, accompanied with another seaman, and for my bowl undertook to transport me; but told me I must be contented to lie down in the keel, and endure much hardship, which I was content to do, to gain my liberty. So they took me aboard, and placed me below in the vessel, in a very uneasy place, and obscured me with boards and other things, where I lay undiscovered, notwithstanding the strict search that was made in the vessel. My two chapmen, who had my bowl, honestly furnished me with victuals daily until we arrived at Lisbon, in Portugal, where (as soon as the master had left the ship, and was gone into the city) they set me on shore, moneyless, to shift for myself. I knew not what course to take, but, as Providence led me, I went up into the city, and came into a fair street; and being weary, I turned my back to a wall, and leaned upon my staff. Over against me were four gentlemen discoursing together. After a while, one of them came to me, and spake to me in a language that I understood not. I told him I was an Englishman, and understood not what he spake. He answered me in plain English, that he understood me, and was himself born near Wisbech, in Lincolnshire: then I related to him my sad condition; and he, taking compassion on me, took me with him, provided for me lodging and diet, and by his interest with a master of a ship bound for England, procured my passage; and bringing me on shipboard, he bestowed wine and strong waters on me, and, at his return, gave me eight stivers, and commended me to the care of the master of the ship, who landed me safe at Dover, from whence I made shift to get to London, where, being furnished with necessaries, I came into the country.

"Thus, honored sir, I have given you a true account of my sufferings, and happy deliverance by the mercy and goodness of God, my most gracious Father in Jesus Christ, my Saviour and Redeemer, to whose name be ascribed all honor, praise, and glory. I conclude, and rest, your worships, in all dutiful respect, WILLIAM HARRISON."

It is difficult to say what amount of credence should be given to this extraordinary narrative. On the one hand it appears impossible to assign a sufficient motive for kidnapping the old man. The persons who attacked him would have been exposed to far less danger of detection had they either murdered him at once, or left him to take his chance of life in the stone pit after the robbery; and much profit was not likely to accrue from the sale of the old man as a slave. On the other hand, it must be remembered that the country was at that time in a disturbed state, and that the risk of detection must not be estimated by what it would be at the present day; that kidnapping was not an uncommon crime; and that no other mode of accounting for Harrison's disappearance has ever been suggested. But be this story true or not, the fact that he had not been murdered is unquestionable. The innocence of the Perrys of the crime for which they had suffered death was established beyond the possibility of doubt; and we have to deal with the fact, a startling one certainly, that John Perry not only sacrificed the lives of two persons with whom he was closely connected, but his own also, to a falsehood which he had no motive whatever for committing.

This opens one of the darkest and strangest pages in the history of human nature. There can be no doubt that he was a victim of that remarkable form of mental disease which induces the sufferer to charge himself and others with imaginary crimes—a malady far more common than ordinary observers suppose. From the earliest periods as to which we have any records, down to the present day, this terrible disease has from time to time presented itself under various forms. The purest minds and the highest intellects have suffered from it no less than the ignorant and the degraded. Indeed, it would seem as if those minds which are most delicately strung, and tuned to the most refined sensibility, are peculiarly liable to its attack. Few men probably have led so pure and innocent a life, or one which afforded so little ground for self-reproval, as the poet Cowper; yet he has told us that "the sense of sin and the expectation of punishment," the "feeling that he had committed a crime"—he knew not what—was ever present to his mind.

There is one incident of this disease, with regard to which those who (as has been the case with ourselves in more instances than one) are brought into contact with the sufferer, should be especially upon their guard. So thoroughly is he convinced of the truth of his story, he narrates it with such earnestness and simplicity, that unless some circumstance has occurred to put the listener upon his guard, it is next to impossible for him to refuse his assent to its truth. As one, who has left a record of the impressions produced on his own mind during the prevalence of delusion, has told us, "of the two, the appearance of the bed, walls, and furniture of his room was false, *not* his preternatural impressions,"* it follows, from this strong internal conviction, that nothing surprises or startles the sufferers. When John Perry was shown the cord which fell from his brother's pocket, had he been fabricating a story he would have paused to consider what he should say, and would very probably have been betrayed into a

* Narrative of the Treatment of a Gentleman during Derangement, 63. 1838.

contradiction or an inconsistency. But his diseased imagination at once seized upon the circumstance as food for the delusion with which his mind was impressed, and wove it into the narrative in a manner which bore the closest possible resemblance to actual truth, because to his mind it was truth.

A case which, in some of its features, bore a striking resemblance to that of the Perrys, is recorded as having happened in the neighborhood of Calais, nearly a century earlier.

A woman disappeared, and suspicion arose that she had been made away with. A man was found lurking in a wood in the neighborhood, and, betraying symptoms of fear and apprehension, he was arrested on suspicion of having murdered her, confessed the crime, and was executed. In two years the woman returned. The heir of the unhappy sufferer sued the judge who had condemned him for damages. They ought not, it was argued, to have condemned any one for the murder until the body had been found, or its absence satisfactorily accounted for; in other words, until the *corpus delicti* had been proved * — a principle well known to our law, and acted upon, in the first instance, in the case of the Perrys, whom Sir Christopher Turner refused to try at the assizes immediately following their apprehension, on this very ground. How the difficulty was got over afterwards does not appear.

It is like calling up spirits from the dead to open

* Annæus Robertus, lib. 1, c. iv.

the stained and faded pages of the old reporters of the proceedings in the Parliament of Paris, or the equally interesting records of trials in our own country, and to read the harangues of forgotten advocates upon interests long gone by, passions long burnt out, and superstitions which the world has outgrown. Nothing is more curious and interesting than to note how, through each change of circumstance and opinion, the human mind remains the same, and to observe the mode in which its delusions shape and accommodate themselves to the prevailing belief of the day, or the particular circumstances by which the patient is surrounded.

In the year 1662, the parish of Aulderne, about midway between Cawdor and Forres, (the scene of Macbeth's interview with the witches) witnessed a very remarkable display of the former kind. "Master Harie Forbes," the minister of the parish, William Dallas, the Sheriff-Depute, and the other magnates of the neighborhood, assembled to receive the full and voluntary confession of Isabell Gowdie. This confession is perhaps the most curious document that is to be found relating to the history of witchcraft. We certainly know of none that is so comprehensive. It is a compendium of the learning on that very curious subject, and it is especially valuable for the internal evidence which it contains, that it was voluntary and sincere—so minute, particular, and earnest is it, that even now it is difficult to keep in mind that it was merely the creation of a diseased brain.

Isabell first met the devil accidentally between

the farmlands of Drumdewin and the sea-shore, but he prevailed upon her to give him an assignation at night in the kirk of Alderne. There they met, Isabell being accompanied by a confidant, one Margaret Brodie. The devil mounted the reader's desk, with a black book in his hand. Isabell renounced her baptism, and putting one hand on the top of her head, and the other on the sole of her foot, made over all between them to the arch-enemy, who thereupon baptized her afresh in his own name. Nothing more occurred at this interview, but it was not long before a second took place, the details of which we must pass over. Isabell was now wholly given up to the devil, and she and her neighbors were employed by him in the commission of crimes of different kinds, up to murder itself. She enumerates those who constituted her company or "covin," to use the technical name; and, curiously enough, the truth of her confessions is confirmed by one at least of her supposed accomplices. There is a wild and picturesque imagination about Isabell Gowdie's confessions, which is not often found in such details. When she describes the mode that was adopted to take away the fruit of the land, she rivals the grotesque power of Callot.

"Before Candlemas," she says, "we went by East Kinloss, and then we yoked a plewghe of paddokis.* The divill held the plewghe, and John Younge in Mebestone, our officer did drywe the plewghe. Paddokis did draw the plewghe as oxen; quickens† were somes; ‡ a riglan's § horn was a cowter;

* Frogs. † Twitch, couchgrass. ‡ Traces. § A ridgel ram.

and a piece of a riglan's horn was a sok. We went two several times about; and all we of the covin went still up and downe with the plewghe praying to the devil for the fruit of that land, and that thistles and briers might grow there."

She visited Fairyland, like Thomas the Rhymer. The Queen of Faerie was "brawli clothed in whyte linens," and the King of Faerie was a "braw man, weill-favored and broad-faced," but she was "affrighted by the elf bulls, which went up and downe thair rowtting and skoylling"; and her information as to that *terra incognita* is but scanty.

Isabell's confession occupied four days. She gives at length the uncouth rhymes by means of which tempests were raised, which enabled her to fly through the air on storms, to change her form for that of a bird, a cat, a hare, or any other animal at will. Her amours with the devil she details with marvelous particularity, and recounts one by one the murders she had committed at his instigation, when she breaks out into this passionate exclamation: "Alace! I deserve not to be sitting hier, for I have done so manie evill deedis, especially killing of men, I deserve to be rievin upon irin harrowes, and worse if it could be devisit!" To the horror of "Master Harie Forbes," he was himself the subject of these terrible incantations. His life was attempted several times.

"Margaret Brodie shot at Mr. Harie Forbes at the standing-stanes, but she missed, and speirit 'if she should shoot again?' And the devil said, 'Not! for we wold nocht get his lyfe at that tyme.' We intentit several tymes for him quhan he was seik. Bessie Hay, Jean Martin the maiden, Bessie Wilson, Margaret Brodie, Elspeth Neshie, and I myself, met in Bessie Wilsones hows, and maid an bag against him. The bag was maid of the flesh, guttis, and gallis of toadis, the liewer of an hear, pickles of corn, and pairingis of naillis of fingers and toes. We steepit all night among water. The divill learned us to saye the wordis following at the making of the bag:

"'He is lying on his bedd, and he is seik and sair,
Let him ly intill that bedd monethes two and dayes thrie mair.
He sal ly intill his bedd, he sal be seik and sair,
He sal ly intill his bedd monethes two and dayes thrie mair.'

And quhan we haid said thes wordis, we wer al on our kneyis, our hair abowt our shoulderis and eyes, holding up our handis to the divill that it might destroy the said Mr. Harie. It was intendit that we, coming into his chalmer in the night-tym, sould swing it on him. And becaus we prevailed not at that tym, Bessie Hay undertook and cam into his chalmer to wisit him, being werie intimat with him, and she brought in of the bag in her handis full of the oil thereof, to have swowng and casten droppis of it on him; but there were some uther worthie persons with him at the tym, by quhich God prevented Bessie Hay that she gat no harm don to him, but swang a litl of it on the bed quhair he lay." *

The confessions conclude with a minute account

* Isabell Gowdie's fourth confession.

of making the image of a child of clay: "It wanted no mark of the image of a bairn, eyes, nose, mouth, litle lippes, and the hands of it folded down by its sydis."

Whilst the clay which formed the image was kneaded, the devil sat on a black "kist," and Isabell and her companions chanted the following rhyme:

"We put this water among this meall,
For long dwying and ill heall;
We put it in intill the fyr,
To burn them up both stik and stour,
That he burnt with our will,
As onie stikill on an kill."

This image represented the child of the Laird of Parkis, "As it was rosted eche other day at the fyr, som tymes on pairt of it, somtymes another, the bairn would be burnt and rosten, even as it was." "Each day we wold water it, and then rost and bak it, and turn it at the fyr, each other day, till that bairn died, and then lay it up, and steired it not until the next bairn was borne; and then within half an yeir efter that bairne was borne, we would take it out of the cradle, and bak it and rost it at the fyr, until that bairn died also.*

"All this and a great manie mor terrible things the said witnesses and notar heard the said Isabell confes, and most willingly and penitently speak furth of her own mouth."

The record is imperfect, but there seems no reason to doubt that Isabell Gowdie and Janet Breadheid suffered at the stake.

*Confession of Janet Breadheid.—See Pitcairn's Criminal Trials, iii, app. vii.

The conviction of guilt was impressed upon their minds as vividly as it was upon that of John Perry, nor can we wonder at the eagerness with which Master Harie Forbes and his confederates pursued these unhappy women to the death. Sir George Mackenzie observes, that in these cases "the accusers are masters or neighbors who had their children dead, and are engaged by grief to suspect these poor creatures. I knew" (he says) "one burnt because a lady was jealous of her with her husband; and the crime is so odious that they are never assisted or defended by their relations. The witnesses and assizes are afraid that if they escape they will die for it, and therefore they take an unwarrantable latitude. And I have observed that scarce ever any who were accused before a country assize of neighbors did escape that trial." *

We are past the age for belief in witchcraft, but the diseased imagination which formerly manifested itself in the wild delusions of poor Isabell Gowdie, now forms for itself a creation far more dangerous, because its phantoms are reconcilable with the ordinary experience of the world. Within the last two years the courts at Westminster were occupied for many days in the investigation of a charge of a most serious nature, brought against a physician by the husband of one of his patients.† The lady kept a journal, in which she noted down with the utmost minuteness the rise, progress, and entire history of

* Mackenzie's Works, ii, 87.

† Robinson *v.* Robinson and Lane; Divorce Court, June 14, 1858, to March 2, 1859.—See *Times*, July 6, 1858.

an overwhelming and passionate attachment between herself and the doctor. This journal came to the husband's hands. The explosion may be imagined. The husband very naturally instituted proceedings for a divorce. When the trial came on, the journal, consisting of three bulky volumes, and extending over a period of five years, was produced. Nothing could be clearer, more explicit, or more astounding, than the disclosures it contained. But there was not a particle of confirmatory evidence to support any one of them; and it was established beyond a doubt that the lady, though apparently conducting herself like other people, and giving no external sign of disordered intellect, was upon this particular subject altogether insane; that the doctor was innocent throughout the affair, and wholly unconscious that he had for years been made the hero of a romance rivaling the adventures of Faublas. This disease sometimes assumes a form even more dangerous than that of self-accusation. A crime is committed, or supposed to have been committed. The details of an inquiry of an exciting nature fill the columns of the press. Presently the imagination fastens upon the circumstances as they are gradually revealed, and the unfortunate patient fancies that he has been a witness of the whole transaction, comes forward believing that he is discharging an imperative duty, and with all the clearness, coolness, and certainty which characterize truth, depones to the creation of his heated brain. A case of this kind occurred at the winter assizes at Stafford, in the year 1857.

The body of a girl named Elizabeth Hopley was found in the canal at Bradley, early on the morning of the 30th of April. There were no marks of violence. About ten o'clock on the previous evening she had left the house of her aunt for the purpose of going to the place where a young man, to whom she was engaged to be married, was in the habit of working. Her road led past the place where her body was found, and it was supposed that, dazzled by the light of some coke-fires, she had missed her way, and fallen over the low wall by which the canal was, at that spot, very insufficiently guarded. About three weeks, however, after the girl's death, a neighbor, of the name of Samuel Wall, declared that Elizabeth Hopley had been murdered, and that he had been present when the crime was committed. A day or two afterwards he was summoned before the magistrates, when he told the following story. He said that on the night of the 29th of April he was on duty as a private watchmen on some premises near a bridge which crossed the railway; that he saw two persons, a man and a woman, on the bridge, and heard a woman's voice say, "Philip, don't kill me! You said you would kill me before!" That the man then raised his hand and struck the woman a violent blow on the head, which knocked her down. Upon this he went up, and instantly recognized the man as one Philip Clare, whom he well knew. He exclaimed, "Philip, you'll have to suffer for this!" Clare turned round and replied, "If you speak, I'll serve you the same!" Clare then lifted the young woman up from the ground, and, followed by Wall, carried her over the railway bridge, and down a road past some cottages, until he came to the canal. Here he paused, and turning round again upon Wall, said, "Now, if you speak or tell any one, I will kill you. I will serve you the same way as I served her, and set some one else to watch instead." He then, in Wall's presence, plunged the woman, who still seemed helpless and insensible, into the canal, close to the spot where, the next morning, her body was discovered.

Wall fixed the time when this occurred as twenty minutes after midnight; and it must be remarked that he was employed as a watchman, and was likely to be habitually observant of the time.

He said that he returned to his employer's premises, being prevented by his fear of Clare from giving any alarm; that after about a quarter of an hour had elapsed, Clare came to him and renewed his threats, when, terrified by the apprehension of immediate violence, he locked himself up in the engine-house until daylight.

Upon this statement, Clare was taken into custody, and committed for trial. At his trial Wall repeated the story he had told the magistrates. There was a total absence of confirmation. It was met by proof that the body showed no sign of having received any blow of the kind described by Wall; that there had been men at work pumping water during the whole night in the immediate neighborhood, who must, in all probability, have heard something, had the affair taken place as Wall described. It was shown, moreover, that from half-past six until about eleven P. M., Clare had been in a public-house at Bilston, which he left, in company with four other men, one of whom accompanied him till within half a mile of his own house. Another witness, a neighbor, proved that about twelve o'clock he met Clare, and entered into conversation with him near his own door; that they remained together until two o'clock next morning. There could not be the slightest doubt of Clare's innocence, and the jury, of course, at once acquitted him. Nor could there be any doubt that Wall believed the story told. The minuteness, the particularity, the graphic details, the conversation, all bear the stamp of that *subjective* truth, which our language has no word to distinguish from *objective* truth. It is curious to observe in how many respects this case resembles that of John Perry. In both there was a period of incubation, during which the mind brooded in silence over its creations; in both the accuser professed to have been present, and thus a participant, though in different degrees, in the crime. In both the conversations with the supposed murderer are minutely detailed; in both the tale is solemnly repeated, consistently, and without variation, at considerable intervals of time, and subject to the test of judicial examination.

A case even more remarkable occurred shortly before the one we have just referred to.

A gentleman of high social position instituted proceedings against his wife with the view of obtaining a divorce.

The innocence of the lady was strongly asserted

and firmly believed. Counter-charges of conspiracy and perjury were brought against the husband and his witnesses. The lady herself was in a state of disordered intellect, produced, as was asserted, by the conduct of the husband, which precluded her from taking any part, or affording any assistance towards her own defense, which, however, was vigorously maintained by friends who were firmly convinced that she was wholly innocent. The inquiry lasted for nearly four years, and at length reached the House of Lords, where the case on behalf of the husband had just terminated when Parliament rose for the Easter recess.

On the House reassembling, there appeared at the bar an elderly and respectable-looking clergyman, who, to the surprise of every one, deposed upon oath that six or seven years before—namely, in the month of May or June, in the year 1849 or '50, he could not say which—he had been an actual eye-witness of the guilt of the lady. He swore that he had never mentioned the circumstance during the six or seven years that had elapsed but to one person, and that person was dead. He had permitted his daughters and his sister to continue on terms of intimacy with the lady whom he accused. He was unable to fix the time of the occurrence, even as to the year in which it took place, or to state who was the partner in her guilt. Every avenue of contradiction was thus cut off, and the story was left to stand or fall, according as the respectable character and social position of the witness, and the apparent conviction with which he told his story, or the improbable nature of that story itself, coupled with the fact that during a most searching investigation, carried on by adverse parties with the utmost eagerness for a period of between four and five years, no circumstance which in the slightest degree corroborated that story had ever come to light, might be considered to be entitled to the greater weight. It was not long, however, before the difficulty was solved. Within a few months, the witness who had given this extraordinary history gave himself up to justice, declaring with every expression of contrition that he had been guilty of forging certain bills of exchange, that they had nearly reached maturity, that he had no means of providing for them, that detection was inevitable, and that he wished to anticipate the blow, and make such reparation as was in his power by a full acknowledgment of his guilt. Upon investigation, it turned out that there was not the slightest foundation for this story; no forgery had been committed—no such bills of exchange had ever been in existence. His delusion as to his own guilt was as complete as his delusion as to that of the lady against whom he had given evidence, over whose strange history he had no doubt brooded for years, until the thick-coming fancies of his brain assumed the form and appearance of substantive creations.

Doctor Southwood Smith, in his "Lectures on Forensic Medicine," after observing how common false self-inculpative evidence is, gives some remarkable instances in which it has occurred. Of these the following is perhaps the most striking:

"In the war of the French Revolution the *Hermione* frigate was commanded by Captain Pigot, a harsh man and a severe commander. His crew mutinied, and carried the ship into an enemy's port, having murdered the captain and many of the officers under circumstances of extreme barbarity. One midshipman escaped, by whom many of the criminals, who were afterwards taken and delivered over to justice one by one, were identified. Mr. Finlaison, the Government actuary, who at that time held an official situation at the Admiralty, states: 'In my own experience I have known, on separate occasions, more than six sailors who voluntarily confessed to having struck the first blow at Captain Pigot. These men detailed all the horrid circumstances of the mutiny with extreme minuteness and perfect accuracy; nevertheless, not one of them had ever been in the ship, nor had so much as seen Captain Pigot in their lives. They had obtained, by tradition, from their messmates, the particulars of the story. When long on a foreign station, hungering and thirsting for home, their minds became enfeebled; at length they actually believed themselves guilty of the crime over which they had so long brooded, and submitted with a gloomy pleasure to being sent to England in irons for judgment. At the Admiralty we were always able to detect and establish their innocence, in defiance of their own solemn asseverations.'"*

We are exhausting our space, though not the number of instances of a similar description which lie

* *London Medical Gazette*, Jan., 1838.

before us, and must content ourselves with one more.

A magistrate of one of the northern counties of England, well known for his active benevolence, during the discharge of his duty as one of the visiting justices of the County Lunatic Asylum, entered into conversation with one of the patients, and was much struck with his rational demeanor and sensible remarks. The man expressed himself grateful for the kindness with which he was treated, and said that he was well aware that it was necessary that he should be under restraint; that although he was perfectly well at that time, he knew that he was at any moment liable to a return of the insanity, during an attack of which he had some years before murdered his wife; and that it would be unsafe to permit him to go at large. He then expressed the deepest contrition for his crime; and after some further conversation the magistrate left him, not doubting the truth of his story. Referring to the case in conversation with the master of the asylum, he expressed much interest, and referred to the patient as "that unhappy criminal lunatic who had murdered his wife"; when to his astonishment, he was informed that the wife was alive and well, and had been to visit her husband only the day before!

We cannot conclude our observations on this interesting subject better than in the words of the old jurist Heineccius:* "Confession is sometimes the voice of conscience. Experience, however, teaches us that it is frequently far otherwise. There

* Exer. 18, § 6.

sometimes lurks, under the shadow of an apparent tranquillity, an insanity which impels men readily to accuse themselves of all kinds of iniquity. Some, deluded by their imaginations, suspect themselves of crimes which they have never committed. A melancholy temperament, the *tædium vitæ*, and an unaccountable propensity to their own destruction, urges some to the most false confessions; whilst they were extracted from others by the dread of torture, or the tedious misery of the dungeon. So far is it from being the fact that all confessions are to be attributed to the stings of conscience, that it has been well said by Calphurnius Flaccus, 'Even a voluntary confession is to be regarded with suspicion'; and by Quintilian, 'a suspicion of insanity is inherent in the nature of all confessions.'"

III.

The Annesley Case.

When the captain of the *Great Britain* ran that unfortunate vessel on to the sands of Dundrum Bay, it was urged in his excuse that so many marvelous tales are told about Ireland, that he was justified in concluding that no obstacle lay in his road from the Isle of Man to New York; that Dublin was as fabulous as Blefuscu; and that the Mourne mountains had no more real existence than the loadstone hill which proved fatal to the ship of Sindbad. The story we are about to tell might almost justify such incredulity; yet it is only one of many equally strange and equally well authenticated.

In the year 1706, Arthur Lord Altham, a needy and dissolute Irish peer, married Mary Sheffield, an illegitimate daughter of the Duke of Buckingham. They lived together for three years; but in 1709 Lord Altham went to Ireland, leaving his wife in England, where she remained until 1713, when she joined her husband in Dublin. From that time until 1716 they resided together, principally at Dunmaine, in the neighborhood of Ross, in the county of Wexford. In 1716 they separated, under circumstances which we shall presently have occasion to notice more minutely, and never met again. In 1717 Lord Altham died, and was succeeded in his title and estates by his brother, Richard Annesley, who remained in undisturbed possession of both for a period of thirteen years. Lady Altham survived her husband for about two years, which were passed in sickness and poverty, but does not appear ever to have taken any step to prevent Richard Annesley's assumption of the character of heir to her husband, to which, of course, he would have had no title if she had a son living at the time of Lord Altham's death. In the year 1739, however, a young man of about four-and-twenty years of age made his appearance in the fleet which, under the command of Admiral Vernon, was lying off Porto-Bello. He called himself James Annesley, stated that he was a son of Lord Altham, that he had been educated and acknowledged as such son until he was nine or ten years of age; that upon the death of his father he had been kidnapped and sold for a slave in America; that he had passed thirteen years in servitude, and at last (after a series of romantic and not very credible adventures, which have nothing to do with our present subject) had effected his escape. Admiral Vernon furnished him with the means of proceeding to England, where he arrived shortly afterwards.

On his arrival in England he went to lodge at Staines, in the neighborhood of Windsor, and here a circumstance occurred which had no doubt a considerable effect on the subsequent proceedings. One of his associates, a man of the name of Redding, was gamekeeper to Sir John Dolbin, the lord of the manor. One morning James Annesley was out with a gun shooting small birds, when Redding called him to assist in capturing a net with which a man of the name of Egglestone was fishing in the river; Annesley's gun unfortunately went off in the scuffle, and mortally wounded Egglestone. There could be little doubt that the discharge of the gun was purely accidental; but Lord Anglesea (for Richard, Lord Altham, had in the meantime succeded to that title also) seized the opportunity to destroy, as he thought, the claimant of his title and estates. He instituted a prosecution against James Annesley for murder; he was prodigal of money and promises amongst the witnesses; and he declared that he would willingly give ten thousand pounds to get him hanged. The jury at the Old Bailey acquitted Annesley, and Lord Anglesea's machinations recoiled upon himself; for there can be no doubt that they greatly influenced both the court and jury against him on the subsequent trial.

On the 11th of November, 1743, the trial for the recovery of the estates came on in the Court of Exchequer in Dublin. It lasted fifteeen days, and above ninety witnesses were examined. The issue between the parties was of the simplest and boldest character. On the one hand, it was asserted that, in the spring of the year 1715, Lady Altham had been delivered at Dunmaine of a son and heir; that all the customary solemnities and rejoicings had taken place; that the child was uniformly acknowledged and treated both by Lord and Lady Altham as their son; that he was shown and spoken of as such to visitors and friends; that when the separation between his parents took place, the mother passionately entreated that she might be permitted to take the child with her, which the father refused, keeping the boy and educating him as the heir to his title and estates. On the other hand, it was denied that Lady Altham ever had a child at all. It was asserted that the very ground of the separation between herself and her husband was the discomfort and disappointment occasioned by her bearing no heir; that it was known to every relation and visitor, to every servant in the house, that Lady Altham never had a child; that the servant who had attended her from her arrival in Dublin to the hour of her death, who had dressed and undressed her every morning and evening, and had never been absent for more than one single week during the whole of that period, was living, and would prove, not only that no child ever was born, but that there never was the slightest chance or probability that Lady Altham would have a child. It is impossible to conceive a simpler issue, or one which might be supposed to be easier for conclusive proof one way or the other; yet two juries came to diametrically opposite conclusions, and so positive is the testimony on each side, that it seems even now, after carefully reading the contradictory evidence which is preserved in upwards of five hundred columns of the State Trials, to be impossible to arrive at any satisfactory result.

It is to be observed that the question raised by this issue was not one of personation or disputed identity. If Lady Altham ever had a son, it was virtually admitted that James Annesley was that son. Nor was the case one of concealed or doubtful marriage, or obscure birth, such as have frequently occupied the courts. From the arrival of Lady Altham in Ireland until her separation from her husband, a period of about three years, they resided publicly together, kept a large establishment of servants, and visited and associated with persons of the most various rank and position in the neighborhood. It seems incredible that any dispute should ever have arisen upon a point so easy of proof as whether persons of their rank, and so circumstanced, had or had not a child; and as we read the evidence adduced, the testimony on the one side seems absolutely conclusive, until it is met by contradictory evidence, to all appearance equally conclusive, on the other.

The household at Dunmaine was large and disorderly, consisting of sixteen or seventeen servants, from the English housekeeper, who was "sent over by my lady," and who rejoiced in the appropriate name of "Mrs. Settright," down to "Smutty, the dog-boy, who was very ugly." Poor Smutty! immortalized by his ugliness. He shows his ill-favored countenance for a moment, and disappears into utter obscurity. Lord Altham had about him, also, a number of hangers-on and humble companions; but, besides these, he associated with gentlemen of his own rank and position; and one of the first witnesses called on behalf of the claimant, was a Major Richard Fitzgerald.

The Major deposed that in the year 1715 he was in the town of Ross, having had occasion to go there on account of some business arising from the death of his uncle, a Mr. Pigott, who lived in the county of Wexford. In Ross he met Lord Altham, who invited him to dinner. The Major excused himself, as he was engaged to dine with some brother officers; "but Lord Altham said deponent must dine with him, and come to drink some groaning drink, for that his wife was in labor. Deponent told him that was a reason he ought not to go; but Lord Altham would not take an excuse, and sent the deponent word the next day to Ross, that *his wife was brought to bed of a son;* and the deponent went to Dunmaine and dined there, and had some discourse about the child, and Lord Altham swore that the deponent should see his son, and accordingly the nurse brought the child to deponent, and deponent kissed the child, and gave half a guinea to the nurse; and some of the company toasted the heir-apparent to Lord Anglesea at dinner. That this was the day after the child was born: and deponent says that he left the country the next day, and went to the county of Waterford, to his own house at Prospect Hall. Says deponent saw the woman to whom he gave the half-guinea, this day of his examination; that he remembers her well, because he took notice of her when he gave her the half-guinea, that she was very handsome; that he did not stay at Dunmaine that night, but came to Ross at nightfall, and was attacked in the road by robbers; that he crossed the ferry on his return home; remembers that Lord Altham was in high spirits with the thoughts of having a son and heir." *

It seems impossible to add to the force of this testimony. No attempt was made to impeach the character or credibility of the witness. Everything concurred to fix the time and circumstances in his mind: mistake appears impossible; and no motive is assignable for willful falsehood. Nor is the evidence given by the next witness less conclusive. John Turner was seneschal to Lord Anglesea. He had lived at Dunmaine for ten years; he had visited Lord Altham; and soon after his own marriage, which took place in December, 1714, he observed appearance of pregnancy in Lady Altham. He says that the next time he saw Lady Altham she told him she had a son; that he afterwards saw the boy, and had him in his arms at Dunmaine when he was about a year and half old; that Lady Altham led the child across the parlor, and Lord Altham kissed him and called him "Jemmy"; that he saw the child subsequently at Ross, and afterwards at Kinnay and Carrickduff, after the separation between Lord and Lady Altham, when he was treated by his father in all respects as his legitimate son; that in the year 1722, meeting Lord Altham at a tavern in Dublin, the boy was sent for, and Lord Altham said to deponent, "You were seneschal to Earl Arthur and Earl John, and you may be seneschal to the child." †

During the eight-and-twenty years that had elapsed between the birth of the child in 1715 and the trial in 1743, it was to be expected that many of

* State Trials, xvii, 1153. † Ibid, xvii, 1154.

those whose evidence would have been most valuable should have died; amongst them were those who stood sponsors for the child at its baptism; Mr. Colclough, Mr. Cliff, and Mrs. Pigott, members of families still holding high positions in the county of Wexford; but the fact of the christening, the rejoicings that took place, the bonfires and festivities, were proved by servants who lived in the house at the time, and proved repeatedly and consistently.

It is impossible within the narrow limits of an article to give even an outline of the evidence of the fifty witnesses who were called to substantiate the claimant's case. It would seem almost needless to strengthen the evidence of Major Fitzgerald and John Turner. Every conceivable confirmation, however, was given. Friends of Lord Altham swore to conversations with him, in which he had spoken in the most open manner of his son, and of the disappointment of his brother's expectations of being his heir. Witnesses were produced who had been present and assisting at the birth of the child; and it is very remarkable that, although these witnesses were drawn from every rank of life, no successful attempt was made to impeach the credibility of any of them, nor was any inconsistency to be discovered in their testimony further than might be satisfactorily accounted for by the long period that had elapsed between the events to which they spoke and the time when they gave their evidence. We now come, however, to the most remarkable conflict of testimony which occurs in the whole case. A woman of the name of Joan Laffan was called. She deposed that she entered Lord Altham's service in 1715; that she was employed as nurse-maid to attend on the child as soon as he came from the wet-nurse; that he was at that time three or four months old, and was in her charge for about a year and a half; that he was treated in all respects as their child by both Lord and Lady Altham, who showed great fondness for him, and into whose bedroom she was in the habit of bringing the child in the morning.

She then gave an account of the separation between Lord and Lady Altham. "It was," she said, "on account of Tom Palliser." "My lord had laid a plot against him, and on one Sunday morning pretended to my lady that he was obliged to go out to dinner. That Mr. Palliser breakfasted with my lord, and they had a bottle of mulled wine for breakfast. As soon as my lord was gone out, Mr. Palliser went into my lady's room, and the plot having been laid before, a signal was made that brought my lord back; that my lord ran up with his sword, and had him brought out of the room, and the groom came to Palliser and said to him, 'Is this the way you keep my lady company?' and took out a case-knife in order to cut his nose, but he was ordered only to cut his ear. *That deponent was standing by in the room, and she had the child in her hand, and he showed her the blood out of Palliser's ear; it was the soft part of the ear that was cut, and the child pointed at the blood that came out of the ear.*"* The same witness deposed that

*State Trials, xvii, 1280.

"she was present when my lord and lady parted; that she saw my lady at the door *with the child in her arms;* that my lord came out of the house in a great rage, and asked where his child was, and upon being told that he was with his mother, he ran up to her and snatched the child out of her arms; that my lady begged very hard she might take the child along with her, but *my lord swore he would not part with the child upon any consideration;* that my lady, finding she could not prevail, burst out a crying, and begged that she might at least give the child one parting kiss; that my lord with some difficulty consented, and my lady drove away to Ross." *

Such is Joan Laffan's story, and we must keep in mind that at a subsequent period it was confirmed by another witness; † but in the meantime, let us turn to Palliser's account of the same transaction.

He stated that when he was very young he spent much of his time at Dunmaine, which was within about three miles of his father's residence, and used to ride Lord Altham's horses hunting. That one day, as they were returning home, Lord Altham told him that he was determined to part with his lady; and upon deponent's asking him his reasons, my lord replied, "I find Lord Anglesea will not be in friendship with me while I live with this woman, *and since I have no child by her I will part with her.*" Palliser then gives an account, in all material circumstances, the same as Joan Laffan's, of his being entrapped by Lord Altham into his wife's room and

* State Trials, xvii, 1168, 1170. † Ibid, 94.

falsely accused of being there for an improper purpose; he takes off his wig and shows the jury where his ear was cut, solemnly asseverates the innocence of Lady Altham, and declares not only that no child was present upon that occasion, but that he "*never saw a child in the house.*" Upon this the court, "apprehending that there was some contradiction between the evidence of Palliser and that of Joan Laffan," as indeed they well might, ordered Laffan to be recalled, and the two witnesses to be confronted. Each repeated the story, each was equally clear, distinct, and positive. We have said that Joan Laffan's evidence was subsequently confirmed by another witness, who deponed to having been present at the parting of Lady Altham and her child. The same is, however, the case with the testimony of Palliser, which was confirmed by Mary Heath, Lady Altham's woman, who went with her in the carriage to Ross, and who swore, most positively, that no such child ever was in existence. It is to be observed that Palliser and Laffan agree that the charge against Lady Altham was false; that Laffan attributes the plot to the revenge of the servants, on account of some mischievous boyish tricks which had been played upon them by Palliser; whilst Palliser himself attributes it to the deeper and more probable motive of a determination on the part of Lord Altham to get rid of a wife from whom he hoped for no heir—a motive which we have seen give rise to some of the darkest domestic tragedies that have disgraced humanity. The case, however, is beset with difficulties on all sides; for if we are to accept the evidence of Palliser as true, the inevitable consequence follows, that we must hold, not only Joan Laffan, but Major Fitzgerald, Turner, and many, indeed most, of the fifty witnesses called on behalf of the claimant, and who swore positively to the existence of the child, to have been deliberately perjured.

After the separation Lady Altham went to reside at Ross, and subsequently removed to Dublin. Her circumstances were extremely narrow, and her health bad, but she was faithfully attended until her death, which took place in October, 1729, by Mary Heath. From her first arrival in Ireland, in 1713, a period of sixteen years, with the exception of a single week, this woman was never absent from her. While she resided at Dunmaine, Heath dressed her every morning and undressed her every night; and this witness swore, in the most distinct and positive manner, that *she never had a child.* It seems to be enough to shake one's confidence in all human testimony to find evidence so clear, distinct, and unimpeachable, on each side; to be compelled to admit that on one side or the other there must be the most willful and deliberate perjury, and yet to feel it impossible to say on which side perjury exists.

Lord Altham removed, shortly after his separation from his wife, to a place called Kinnay, in the county of Kildare, and the issue now assumes a different aspect. It is admitted that there was a child at Kinnay; that he was put to school by Lord Altham, and treated as part of his family; but it is contended that he was the illegitimate child of Lord Altham, by a woman of the name of Joan Landy, who had been a servant in the house at Dunmaine, and that he had been brought to the house subsequently to Lady Altham's departure.

In the earlier part of the case the claimant is met with the general denial—Lady Altham never had a son. Prove that she had, and we will admit you to be that son. In the latter part, the defendant says in substance—I admit that, during Lord Altham's residence at Kinnay, there was a boy who passed as his son. I admit that you are that boy; but you are not the heir of Lord Altham, but his illegitimate son by Joan Landy.

The whole of the evidence, therefore, changes its character: when Mary Heath swears that her mistress never had a child, whilst Eleanor Murphy swears that both she and Heath were present at the birth, one or the other must be perjured. But Lord Altham might use expressions as to "little Jemmy," which one witness might understand as being a distinct declaration of his legitimacy, and another might think only conveyed the expression of his affection for his natural child.

During the first period the existence of the child is denied; during the second it is admitted; and we shall now proceed to follow the fortunes of the boy, waiving for the present the question of who was his mother.

Lord Altham, after his separation from his wife, formed a connection with one Miss Gregory, who seems to have exercised an unbounded influence over him. After a short time poor "Jemmy" was turned out to wander in rags about the streets of Dublin. Here, however, he met with friends: a good-natured student in Trinity College, of the name of Bush, clothed and fed him, and employed him to run errands, till his grandfather told him it was not fit he should have a lord for his servant, when he was turned out upon the world again. He was next taken charge of by an honest butcher named Purcell, who took him home and brought him up with his own son. Purcell tells the court that whilst "the boy was in his house, a gentleman (who was then called Richard Annesley, and is the now defendant, the Earl of Anglesea) came to deponent's house and asked if one Purcell did not live there, and said he supposed they sold liquors; that the gentleman had a gun in his hand, and sat down, and having called for a pot of beer, asked deponent if he had a boy in his house called James Annesley? To which deponent answered that there was such a boy in the house, and called his wife and told her that a gentleman wanted to see the boy; says that the child was sitting by the fireside, and immediately saw Mr. Richard Annesley, though he could not see the child by reason of the situation where he sat; says the child trembled and cried, and was greatly affrighted, saying, 'That is my uncle Dick'; says that when the child was shown to the defendant, he said to Jemmy, 'How do you do?' That the child made his bow, and replied, 'Thank God, very well.' That the defendant then said, 'Don't you know me?' 'Yes,' said the child, 'you are my uncle Annesley.' That thereupon the defendant told the deponent that the child was the son of Lord Altham, who lived at Inchcore; to which deponent replied, 'I wish, sir, you would speak to his father to do something for him.'" *

The child's fear of his uncle was not without good cause. About three weeks after Lord Altham's death, Richard Annesley came a second time to seek for the child, and desired it should be sent to one Jones in the market. Purcell suspected mischief. The honest butcher shall tell his story in his own words: "Then deponent took a cudgel in one hand, and the child in the other, and went to the said Jones's house, when he saw the present Earl of Anglesea, (who was then in mourning) with a constable and two or three other odd-looking fellows attending about the door; that deponent took off his hat, and saluted my lord, which he did not think proper to return; but as soon as he saw the child in the deponent's hands, he called to a fellow that stood behind deponent's back, and said to him, 'Take up that thieving son of a ——, (meaning the child) and carry him to the place I bid you.' After some more language of the same kind from his lordship, the deponent said, 'My lord, he is no thief; you shall not take him from me; whoever offers to take him from me I'll knock his brains out'; then deponent took the child (who was trembling with fear) and put him between his legs." †

Some high words passed, but the butcher was true to his trust; the lord and the constable sneak-

* State Trials, xvii, 1201. † Ibid, xvii, 1202.

ed off, and the child was carried back in safety. He was not long so fortunate. Fear of a repetition of the attempt to capture him induced him, very foolishly, to leave his friend the butcher. He then took refuge in the house of a Mr. Tigh; but it was not long before the emissaries of his uncle discovered his retreat, forced him into a boat, and on board a ship bound for Philadelphia, which sailed on April, 1728. His uncle himself placed him in the ship, and returned to Dublin, thinking, no doubt, that he had heard the last of him. All the details of this nefarious transaction are given with the utmost minuteness, and without shame or hesitation, by the very agents who were employed in it. The share which Lord Anglesea took in the abduction of his brother's child is hardly disputed. The contention is confined to the point that the child was illegitimate. The villany of the act seems never to have struck any of the parties concerned. But this act appears to us to turn the wavering balance of evidence against Lord Anglesea. If this boy were really the son of Joan Landy, it could not be difficult for Lord Anglesea to procure proof of that fact whilst the events were so recent, whilst Lady Altham was still living, and when he had himself, by common consent, been admitted to the title and estates of his brother. If, on the other hand, he knew that the boy was his brother's legitimate son, he had the strongest interest to remove him out of the way before any inquiries could be made, and whilst he was in the obscurity into which his father had permitted him to fall.

Yet a suspicion, almost equally strong, against the truth of the claimant's case, would seem to arise from the fact that Joan Landy was living, and yet was never called.

The claimant's story was, that this woman was his nurse; that her own child, which was a few months older than himself, had died, when he was four or five years old, of small-pox. Who could be so valuable a witness for the claimant as this woman? Yet she was never examined, nor was her absence ever satisfactorily accounted for. If it is argued that she might have been called by either side—that it was equally open to the defendant to produce her to negative, as to the claimant to produce her to support the story—it may be answered, that she could hardly be expected to come forward to denounce her own son as an impostor. The non-production of a witness, who must have important evidence in her power, who was naturally the witness of the claimant, and whose absence is not satisfactorily accounted for, throws the gravest suspicion upon his whole case. To what conclusion, then, can we come? The jury, after a consultation of about two hours, found for the claimant. They must therefore have considered Heath, Palliser, Rolph, and the other witnesses who swore to the non-existence of the child, to have perjured themselves. The plaintiff appears to have been disposed to follow up his victory, for an indictment for perjury was at once preferred against Mary Heath. The same evidence was repeated; Joan Laffan was again examined. But the jury found her "Not guilty." They must therefore have considered that Laffan, and all those who swore to Lady Altham having had a child, had been guilty of the crime of which they acquitted Heath. James Annesley does not appear to have taken any further steps to obtain possession of the estates and honors to which the decision of the jury had established his title. He died at Blackheath on the 2d of January, 1760. His uncle, Richard Annesley, Lord Anglesea, closed his career of profligacy and cruelty twelve short months afterwards. James Annesley left a son, who died an infant, and a daughter, who married, and whose children died young. Thus his line became extinct, and his rights, whatever they were, reverted to his uncle. Such was the termination of the "Annesley Case," memorable for the dark mystery in which it must forever remain shrouded, and for the curious picture which it affords of the manners and habits of life that prevailed little more than a hundred years before our own day.

IV.

Eliza Fenning.

Immediately adjoining to High Holborn, and parallel with the southern side of Red Lion Square, runs a long, narrow, gloomy lane, called Eagle Street. Sickly children dabble in the gutters, and gaze wistfully at the sugar-plums and hard-bake, painfully suggestive of plaster of Paris and cobbler's wax, which are displayed in the windows of the better class of shops, in company with farthing prints of theatrical characters, pegtops, battledores, and other objects of attraction to the youth of London. Vendors of tripe and cats'-meat, rag and bottle dealers, marine-store keepers; merchants who hold out temptations in prose and verse, adorned with apoplectic numerals, to cooks and housemaids to purloin dripping, kitchen stuff, and old wearing apparel; barbers who "shave well for a halfpenny," shoe-vampers, fried-fish sellers, a coal and potato dealer, and a bird-stuffer, share the rest of the street with lodging-houses of the filthiest description.

In the month of July, 1815, a remarkable scene was witnessed in this lane. In a back room of the house No. 14 (since pulled down to make way for Day & Martin's blacking manufactory) the body of a young woman, who had a few days before been executed at Newgate for poisoning the family in which she was cook, with arsenic, was exhibited by her parents to all comers. The street was filled with crowds of compassionate or inquisitive gazers. Money was freely given and readily received. This extraordinary exhibition continued for five days. On the 31st of July, a funeral procession wound its way up Lamb's Conduit Street, to the burial-ground at the back of the Foundling Hospital. The pall was borne by six young women robed in white. Thousands of spectators (it is stated, in the papers of the day, as many as ten thousand) followed the coffin to the grave, and crowded round as it was lowered into the earth. It bore upon its lid these words—"Elizabeth Fenning, died July 26, 1815, aged 22 years." From that day to this, the case of Eliza Fenning has been cited as one in which an innocent person fell a victim to the hasty judgment of a prejudiced and incompetent tribunal. Nor must it be supposed that this feeling has been confined to an ignorant or angry populace. Sir Samuel Romilly recorded his belief in her innocence. Curran was in the habit of declaiming in glowing words on the injustice of her fate; and even recently an able and kind-hearted man, whose experience of criminal inquiries was most extensive, and certainly not of a kind to induce him lightly to assume the innocence of a convicted felon, has told the story of Eliza Fenning, and concludes his narrative in the following words: "Poor Eliza Fenning! So young, so fair, so innocent, so sacrificed! Cut down even in thy morning, with all life's brightness only in its dawn! Little did it profit thee that a city mourned over thy early grave, and that the most eloquent of men did justice to thy memory." *

On the other hand, it must be remembered that Fenning was defended by able counsel; that after her conviction the case was again investigated by the law advisers of the Crown; that the trial took place on the 11th of April, and the execution was delayed until the 26th of July—a period of more than three months, during which time every opportunity was afforded for bringing forward any circumstance that might tell in the prisoner's favor; that the result of this inquiry, the patience and impartiality of which there seems to be no reasonable ground to doubt, was a confirmation of the verdict of the jury. Here then, we find the remarkable fact, that in a case unattended by any of those circumstances which would be likely to excite popular sympathy on the one hand, or to pervert the judgment of the ordinary tribunals on the other, there is a distinct issue between the decision of the law and the verdict of public opinion. It speaks well both for the people and for the tribunals by which justice is administered, that such a case is of extreme rarity; and it is an interesting and curious inquiry to examine the facts from which it arises.

Eliza Fenning was cook in the family of a Mr. Robert Gregson Turner, a law stationer in Chancery Lane. The family consisted of Turner, his wife, two apprentices named Gadsden and King—youths of seventeen or eighteen years of age, who lived in the house—a housemaid of the name of Sarah Peer,

*Vacation Thoughts on Capital Punishments, by Charles Phillips; p. 102.

and the prisoner. Turner's father, Mr. Orlibar Turner, was a partner in the business, but resided at Lambeth. On Tuesday, the 21st of March, Orlibar Turner dined with his son and his daughter-in-law. Part of the dinner consisted of some yeast dumplings, of which all three partook. They had hardly done so when they were attacked by violent pain, accompanied by the symptoms of arsenical poisoning. Soon afterwards, Gadsden, one of the apprentices, who had dined at an earlier hour, came into the kitchen, and finding the remains of the dumplings, which had been brought down from the parlor, ate a small piece, when he was attacked by similar symptoms. The next sufferer was Eliza Fenning herself, who was taken ill in a like manner later in the afternoon. Sarah Peer and King, the other apprentice, who had dined earlier and did not eat any part of the dumplings, escaped.

The first inquiry is, in what medium was the poison conveyed?

All the persons who had partaken of the dumplings were attacked in a greater or less degree. The flour from which they were made was examined, but no poison found; and Fenning, Peer, and King had dined on a pie, the crust from which was made of the same flour, without any ill effects. The poison, therefore, was not in the flour. Some sauce had been served in a boat separate from the dumplings, and of this sauce Mr. Orlibar Turner did not partake, yet he was one of the sufferers. The poison, therefore, was not in the sauce; nor was it in the yeast, the remains of which were also examined.

There was what would now be considered a most unaccountable amount of carelessness in the examination of the dumplings themselves; but the remains of the dough left in the pan in which they were prepared was examined, and unquestionably contained arsenic. Indeed, no reasonable ground has ever been suggested for doubting that the poison was contained in the dumplings, and that it was placed there by some one during their preparation.

The next inquiry is, how was the poison procured?

Mr. Turner had been in the habit of using arsenic for the destruction of rats and mice, with which his house was infested; and the poison was kept with the most culpable negligence. It lay in an open drawer in the office, unlocked, and in which waste paper was kept. It was urged that Fenning was in the habit of taking paper from the drawer for the purpose of lighting the fire, and an inference was sought to be drawn from that circumstance unfavorable to her. It is manifest that nothing could be more groundless. The arsenic was no doubt obtained from the drawer—the packet in which it was kept having been missed a few days before; but there was not one particle of evidence, with regard to the abstraction of the arsenic, affecting Fenning more than any other member of the family; for to that drawer all the persons in the house had easy access.

Fenning had been in the service about seven weeks. Soon after she entered it, her mistress observed some levity of conduct on her part towards the apprentices, and reproved her severely for it, threatening to discharge her; but this passed over; and with this exception, she does not appear to have had any discomfort or ground of ill-will against her mistress, or any others of the family. We look in vain, therefore, for any adequate motive for so horrible a crime. We must now trace the few circumstances, and they are very few, which the jury considered sufficient to lead them to the conclusion of the guilt of the prisoner.

On the morning of the 20th of March, some yeast was brought to the house by the brewer's man, which had been ordered by Fenning, without the knowledge of her mistress, a day or two before. The yeast was received by Sarah Peer, the housemaid, who poured it into a white basin, and gave it to Fenning. The remains of the yeast was afterwards examined, and found to be perfectly pure. On Tuesday morning, the 21st of March, Mrs. Turner went into the kitchen and gave Fenning directions as to preparing the dumplings. Fenning kneaded the dough, made the dumplings, was in the kitchen the whole time until they were served up to table, and during the greater part of that time was there alone—Mrs. Turner having left her soon after giving her orders, and Sarah Peer, the housemaid, being engaged at her duties in other rooms. Fenning, therefore, had ample opportunity to mix the poison with the dumplings; and it is difficult to suppose that any other person could have meddled with them without her being aware of the fact. Indeed, she herself stated that no other person had anything to do with the dumplings.* On the remains of the dinner being brought down into the kitchen, Gadsden, as we have before stated, came in, and seeing one of the dumplings, took up a knife and fork and was going to eat it, when Fenning exclaimed, "Gadsden, do not eat that: it is cold and heavy; it will do you no good." Gadsden, in his evidence, adds: "I ate a piece about as big as a walnut, or bigger. There was a small quantity of sauce in the boat: I took a bit of bread and sopped it in it, and ate that." † Gadsden was taken ill about ten minutes afterwards. He was not, however, too ill to be sent for the elder Turner's wife, Mrs. Margaret Turner. On her arrival, she found her husband, son, and daughter-in-law extremely ill; and very soon afterwards Eliza Fenning herself was attacked with similar symptoms. Here, then, we find this curious fact—all the persons who have partaken of the dumplings at dinner are ill: Gadsden is warned by Fenning not to eat them; he neglects the warning, and is almost immediately taken ill in the same manner; he is sent to Lambeth to fetch Mrs. Margaret Turner; and Fenning is not taken ill until after her arrival. Considering the distance from Chancery Lane to Lambeth, this must have been a considerable interval. As the effects of the poison (even when taken in so small a quantity as by Gadsden) were almost immediate, it follows that Fenning did not take it until some time after these symptoms were apparent in the others, and subsequent to the warning she gave Gadsden. This

* 71*st* Q.

† Short-hand copy of the Trial, 8*th* Q.

seems to dispose of the arguments in favor of her innocence, which have been founded on the fact of her having been herself a sufferer from the poison. What might be her motive is a matter involved in great obscurity; but there seems to be no doubt that she took it, for some reason or other, after she had seen its effects, and after she had seen cause to warn Gadsden against the dumplings.

This very slender evidence is all that exists apart from that which is derived from Fenning's own statements, which we shall consider presently.

It amounts to little more than proof that Fenning might easily have committed the crime, and that it is difficult to suppose that any other person could. The poison was unquestionably in the dumplings; it was unquestionably placed there during their preparation. Who but Fenning could have done this? But we now come to the consideration of what appears to us to be by far the most important evidence in the case—namely, the statements made by Eliza Fenning herself.

Mrs. Turner the elder arrived at the house, as we have seen, in the afternoon. She is asked whether she had any conversation with Fenning on the subject:

"*90th Q.*—Did you say anything to her while you were there that day respecting the dumplings?

"*A.*—I exclaimed to her, 'Oh, these devilish dumplings!' supposing they had done the mischief. She said, '*Not the dumplings, but the milk, madam.*' I asked her, 'What milk?' she said, 'The halfpennyworth of milk that Sally had fetched to make the sauce.'

"*91st Q.*—Did she say who had made the sauce?

"*A.*—My daughter. I said, 'That cannot be—it could not be the sauce.' She said, 'Yes; Gadsden ate a very little bit of dumpling, not bigger than a nut, but licked up three parts of a boat of sauce with a bit of bread.'"

During the whole of the next day, Fenning, in reply to repeated inquiries, persisted that the poison was in the milk which was fetched by Sarah Peer, and used for the sauce; that it was not in the dumplings; and that no one had mixed anything in the dumplings, or had anything to do with them, but herself. (*Q. 69, 70, 71.*)

We have already adverted to the fact that Mr. Turner, who did not partake of the sauce, (*94th Q.*) was as ill as any of the others. This is, of course, conclusive of the fact that the poison was not in the sauce, or at any rate, not in the sauce alone.

The arguments in favor of the innocence of Fenning have been almost entirely based on the fact that she herself partook of the poisoned dumplings. As we have already seen, she did not do this until after the effects had been produced upon all the other sufferers, and after she had warned Gadsden that the dumpling was "cold and heavy, and would do him no good." Now, in order to support the hypothesis of her innocence, it must be supposed that, feeling certain that she had mixed no deleterious article in the dumplings, that no other person could have done so, she eats a portion of them to prove her conviction of that fact; otherwise, why, when she had dined a short time before on beefsteak-pie, should she eat the "cold and heavy" dumpling which she had warned Gadsden not to meddle with? She is then immediately taken ill. Supposing she were innocent, her first exclamation would have been one of surprise. "The dumplings are poisoned! who has done this?" Instead of this, she seeks to divert suspicion from the dumplings, and to cast it upon the milk which had been fetched by Sarah Peer.

This ready falsehood, and attempt to divert the suspicion which was pointing at her towards an innocent person, appears to us to afford strong evidence of her guilt; and this evidence is strengthened by the fact that even in her falsehood she was not consistent. The next day, when she was taken into custody, she changed her story. We find no more about the milk. She tells the constable that she thinks the poison was in the yeast, that she saw a red settlement in it. We have already stated that the remains of the yeast were examined, and nothing whatever of a deleterious nature discovered. On her trial she abandoned both these stories, and confined herself to a general assertion of her innocence, in which she persisted on the scaffold.

Such, then, are the facts proved in evidence in the case of Eliza Fenning. We have purposely abstained from alluding to the utterly irrelevant matter with which the papers of the day were filled. On the one side, Eliza Fenning was represented as a paragon of beauty and virtue; on the other, as a monster of depravity and vice. There is not one particle of reason for believing either one statement or the other. Until she was charged with the crime for which she suffered, she seems to have been very much like any other commonplace servant of a somewhat low class. Is there, then, evidence sufficient to lead us, after a dispassionate consideration, to a conclusion either one way or the other? We confess that we think there is; and the conclusion at which we arrive is, that Fenning was guilty.

By a process of exhaustion we arrive at the fact that it was hardly possible that any person but Fenning could have introduced the arsenic into the dumplings. This, alone, would perhaps not justify us in coming to a positive conclusion; but her own conduct, her false and contradictory statements, her warning Gadsden, and her eagerness to throw the blame on a person who was undoubtedly innocent, leave in our minds no doubt of her own guilt.

We are met, however, by two difficulties. First, the absence of any adequate motive for the crime; and, secondly, the fact that she herself partook of the poisoned dumplings.

With regard to the first, all persons who have any practical experience of criminal courts know how slight and insignificant are the motives which sometimes impel to the commission of the most appalling crimes. The poisoning even of children by their own parents, to obtain the paltry allowance made by burial-clubs on their deaths, became so common a few years ago as to occasion the express interference of the legislature. We were ourselves present at the trial of Betty Eccles. That wretched woman had contracted a habit of poisoning. If a neighbor's child cried, it was quieted with a dose of arsenic. One poor little victim, not suspecting the cause of her agony, besought the murderess to take her to the pump to get a drink of water, to allay the burning thirst with which she was tormented; "Thee mayest lie where thee art," was the reply; "thee won't want water long." When incendiary fires were rife, many instances occurred in which there seemed to be no assignable motive at all beyond the mere desire to see a blaze and to cause an excitement.

The genius of Scott was never displayed in greater vigor than in the scene where Elspeth of the Craigburnfoot discloses to Lord Glenallan the conspiracy which resulted in the death of Eveline Neville; nor is his knowledge of the human heart more completely shown by anything than the trivial cause which he assigns for Elspeth's bitter hatred and deep revenge: "I hated Miss Eveline Neville for her ain sake. I brought her frae England, and during our whole journey she gecked and scorned at my northern speech and habit, as her southland leddies and kimmers had done at the boarding-school, as they ca'd it." Most of our readers, we fear, if they look honestly back through their own experience, will be able to recall some domestic tragedy which has originated in as trivial a cause. It is equally true of crime as of other things, moral and physical, that the most monstrous growth often springs from the most minute seed.

With regard to the second argument, it must be owned that, if the dumplings had been prepared for the dinner of which Fenning was to partake, it would have been one of considerable force. But this was not so. Fenning had prepared the dinner for herself, her fellow-servant, Gadsden, and the other apprentice. She made the crust of the pie from the same flour which was used for the dumplings, but no one suffered from sharing that meal. She ate the dumpling after the ill effects had been experienced — after she had cautioned Gadsden. Whether she ran the risk for the sake of concealing her crime, or whether she desired to destroy her own life, it is impossible to say. It has been asserted that, after the execution of Fenning, some person confessed that he had been the murderer. This rests on mere rumor. We have reason to believe that there is more ground for the statement which has also been made, that though Eliza Fenning persisted in the assertion of her innocence in public and to the Ordinary of Newgate, yet that she confessed her guilt to another person. Neither of these reports, however, have ever assumed a tangible form, or one which would enable them to be submitted to that kind of scrutiny which alone could give them value. We have therefore disregarded them altogether in considering the case, and confined our attention to legitimate evidence alone. We attach but little value to Fenning's assertion of her innocence on the scaffold. Few weeks have passed since Mullins was executed, making similar protestations; yet we presume that no doubt exists in the mind of any sane man that he was the murderer of Mrs. Emsley. Gleeson Wilson, the murderer of

Mrs. Hendrickson and her children, persisted to the last in asseverations of his innocence.

We have said that it is rarely that public opinion fails to confirm the decisions of our criminal courts. We attribute this most happy circumstance mainly to three things: the publicity of all judicial proceedings; the placing of all issues of fact in the hands of the jury; and the freedom of the judge from any part in the conduct of the trial. But we shall probably startle many of our readers when we say that, in one most important particular, we think that one of the oldest and best established rules of our criminal law might be considerably modified with advantage to the ends of justice. We allude to the rule which, under all circumstances, prohibits the examination of a person charged with crime, and the correlative or complimentary rule which precludes him from giving evidence in his own behalf. No rule is more strictly observed in English jurisprudence. From the moment that a man is charged with crime until he is placed at the bar for trial, he is hedged round with precautions to prevent him from criminating himself. Upon his trial he cannot be asked to explain a doubtful or suspicious circumstance. Whether he will or not, his mouth is closed, except for the purpose of cross-examining the witnesses, until all the evidence is heard against him, and then he addresses the jury with the disadvantage (and, supposing him to be innocent, it is a very serious disadvantage) that even the jury or the judge cannot put any question to him which might enable him to clear up what was obscure, or to explain what might appear to be suspicious in his conduct. The armor with which the law thus shields the guilty becomes an incumbrance upon the innocent.

The rule originates, no doubt, in a love of fair play. Every man is entitled to be considered innocent until he is proved to be guilty. You must not make a man criminate himself. These are aphorisms in which we fully agree. But it is equally true that you ought to give every man the utmost freedom to prove that he is innocent, and to exculpate himself.

We are fully aware of the evils that arise from the system pursued in the French courts, where the judge interrogates the culprit (we use the word in its legal sense of an *accused* person, not in its popular meaning of a *guilty* one) where the grave judicial inquiry degenerates into a "keen encounter of their wits," and the hand which ought to hold the balance steady wields, instead, the sword of the combatant. We know, too, the still greater evils that attend the system of secret examination by the judge, which prevails in other Continental States, and with which the readers of Feuerbach are familiar; and we would far rather retain the imperfections of our own system than adopt the infinitely worse mischiefs which are attendant upon either. Still, the reverse of wrong is not necessarily right; and our own course of proceeding might, we think, be modified with advantage.

In the present state of the law this curious anomaly exists, that in the very same state of facts, it depends upon whether the proceeding is civil or criminal, whether the mouth of the accused person is closed or not. A and his wife, walking home at night, are met by B and his wife, when B knocks A down. A indicts B for the assault, and this being a criminal proceeding, A and his wife give their evidence upon oath, whilst neither B nor his wife can be examined at all. But suppose that, instead of indicting B, A had brought an action against him, the whole case is changed. Now A and B, and their respective wives, can all be examined and cross-examined. Can there be a doubt which course is most conducive to the elucidation of the truth; and can a grosser absurdity be conceived than that the same court should adopt modes of procedure so inconsistent in an inquiry into the same facts, before the same judge and the same jury, and practically between the same parties?

A case occurred last summer which excited great interest, and which forcibly illustrates the evil we complain of.

A clergyman of the name of Hatch was indicted for a gross offense alleged to have been committed upon a child of tender years, who had been intrusted to his care as a pupil. The charge rested almost solely on the evidence of the child, a girl of the name of Eugenia Plummer. Neither Hatch nor his wife could be examined, and, as theirs was the only testimony by which, from the nature of the case, the charge could be rebutted, Hatch was convicted. Under the circumstances, it was hardly possible that the jury could come to any other conclusion. A few weeks elapsed, and Eugenia Plummer was placed at the same bar, charged with perjury. Then the tables were turned. Hatch and his wife were examined; the child's mouth was closed. The jury convicted Eugenia Plummer of perjury. On the evidence before the jury no other result could reasonably have been expected. Both the juries discharged their duties with honesty and intelligence. Both were assisted in their deliberations by judges of the highest character and the greatest experience and ability, yet one jury or the other convicted an innocent person. If Plummer was guilty, Hatch was innocent; if Hatch was guilty, Plummer was herself the double victim of his brutality and his perjury. We express no opinion whatever as to which jury was right, but it is manifest that both could not be. It must, we think, be clear to every one, that the only way in which a case of this kind could be satisfactorily tried must be by confronting and examining both the parties. To attempt to try such issues separately is like trying to cut a knot with the two disunited halves of a pair of scissors.

If, upon one trial, both could have been examined, the inquiry would very possibly have terminated in the acquittal of both. In other words, the jury might have found the evidence of both so unsatisfactory that they could not found any decision upon it. Such a result, certainly, would not have been desirable, yet it would have been far less objectionable than what has actually taken place. The conviction of Eugenia Plummer for perjury has operated as a virtual acquittal of Hatch.

But every one must feel that that acquittal, having been obtained when the mouth of the only material witness against him was closed, is far less satisfactory than it would have been if it had resulted from the decision of a jury who had heard the evidence of Plummer.

The case of Elizabeth Canning, which we examined at length in a former number, was of the same description. Squires was convicted of felony on the evidence of Canning, and Canning was subsequently convicted of perjury committed in that very evidence. On the first trial Squires could not be examined; on the second, Canning was silenced, and both the accused persons were convicted. Such cases are of frequent occurrence, and they are always attended by this evil, that, whether rightly or not, public opinion will unavoidably be divided as to the result. The conviction of Canning hardly diminished either the number or the zeal of those who had espoused her cause; and it would probably be found that the juries who came to conflicting decisions in the cases of Hatch and Eugenia Plummer, represent, not unfairly, the diversities of public opinion.

The remedy we would suggest is, that in all cases a culprit should be permitted to tender himself for examination. We think that to allow the prosecutor to call the culprit, and to examine him whether he would or no, would be attended with evils greater than any advantage to be derived from such a course—evils less in degree, though the same in kind, as those which make us shrink with horror from the idea of extracting even truth by the means of torture—means which have never been used in our courts since they were adopted by the express command of that queen whom Lord Macaulay has held up to us as the pattern of every gentle and feminine virtue, and her ruthless husband. If an accused person choose to remain silent, or to make his statement to the jury without the sanction of an oath, and without submitting its truth to the test of cross-examination, he should be fully at liberty to do so, subject, of course, to the unfavorable effect which such a proceeding would unavoidably have on the minds of the jury. That this would be the line taken by the guilty would no doubt frequently be the case; but every innocent man would, we believe, gladly adopt the other course. We have heard it urged that the ignorant, the stupid, or the timid man would be thus placed at a disadvantage when exposed to the cross-examination of an experienced, acute, and possibly not very scrupulous counsel. We believe, on the contrary, that such a person is the very one to whom (supposing him to be innocent) the course we suggest would be of the greatest advantage. What is the position of such a man now? He is left to blunder his story out as best he may, casting it before the jury in a confused, unintelligible mass, with, very possibly, the most material parts wholly omitted. If our suggestion were adopted, the thread of his narrative would be drawn from the tangled skein by the hand of an experienced advocate—its consistency and its truth would be tested by cross-examination, and confirmed by re-examination. A greater boon to the ignorant or timid man falsely accused of crime, than such a mode of exculpating himself, we can hardly conceive.

The ultimate object of all criminal jurisprudence is the safety of society. When a crime is committed, especially if it is one of a nature to excite extreme horror and detestation, the first and most natural impulse is to fix the guilt upon some one. Outraged humanity and public indignation demand a victim. In the case of the Road murder, we have seen persons who, from their position and education, ought to know better, calling out for the abandonment of the established forms of law and justice and the adoption of some new and inquisitorial mode of proceeding. We have seen a magistrate holding a sort of extrajudicial court, listening to, and even asking for, the most absurd and irrelevant gossip, and exposing the gravest and most serious inquiry to ridicule.

To attempt to supply a defect by adopting an exceptional course of proceeding in an individual case, would only be to introduce a mischief of far greater magnitude. It is far better that an individual crime, however horrible, should remain unpunished, than that rules established for the purposes of justice should be strained or set aside. But it is well that we should consider carefully whether those rules rest on a sound foundation. We have, with great advantage, abandoned the rule which formerly excluded the parties to civil suits from giving evidence. We believe that nothing but good would result from the removal of the anomaly which still exists in our criminal courts when the accuser is sworn, and gives his evidence on oath, whilst the accused is refused the same sanction to his denial of the charge.

V.

Spencer Cowper's Case.

At the summer assizes at Hertford, on the 16th of July, 1699, a young barrister, rising into eminence in his profession, the son of a baronet of ancient family, who was one of the representatives, and a brother of a King's Counsel, who was the other representative of the town in Parliament, held up his hand at the bar to answer a charge of murder. It was not for blood shed in an angry brawl—it was not for vindicating his honor by his sword in defiance of the law, that Spencer Cowper was arraigned. He was accused of having deliberately murdered a woman, whose only fault was having loved him too devotedly and trusted him too implicitly. He was called upon to plead to a charge which, if proved, would not only consign his body to the gibbet, but his name to eternal infamy.

Sarah Stout was the only daughter of a Quaker maltster in the town of Hertford. Her father was an active and influential supporter of the Cowpers at the elections, and the kind of intimacy which ordinarily takes place under such circumstances arose between the families. Attentions, no doubt highly flattering to their vanity, were paid to the wife and daughter of the tradesman by the ladies of the baronet's family; and an intimacy arose between Spencer Cowper and Sarah, which did not cease when she was left an orphan upon the death of her father, and he became the husband of another woman. He managed the little fortune which had been bequeathed to her; he occasionally took up his abode (whether as a guest or lodger does not appear) at her mother's house, when business called him to Hertford; and he unhappily inspired her with a violent, and, as the event proved, a fatal passion.

Never did the truth of the proverb, "Cucullus non facit monachum," or rather, in this case, *monacham*, receive a stronger confirmation than from the story of poor Sarah Stout. Stormy passions beat under the dove-colored bodice, and flashed from the eyes which were shaded by the close white cap and poke bonnet of the Quakeress. Her whole heart and soul were given to Spencer Cowper. A man of sense and honor would, under such circumstances, at once have broken off the connection, and saved the girl, at the cost of some present suffering, from future guilt and misery. A man of weak determination and kind feelings might have got hopelessly involved in attempting to avoid inflicting pain. Cowper did neither. He carried on a clandestine correspondence with her under feigned names, and received letters from her breathing the most ardent passion, which he displayed amongst his profligate associates. He introduced a friend to her as a suitor, and then betrayed to that friend the secrets which, above all others, a man of honor is bound to guard with the strictest fidelity. He behaved as ill as a man could do under the circumstances.

On the morning of Monday, the 13th day of March, the first day of the spring assizes of 1699, Spencer Cowper arrived in Hertford, traveling (as was then the custom of the bar) on horseback. He went direct to the house of Mrs. Stout, where he was expected, in consequence of a letter which had been written, announcing his intended visit. He was asked to alight, but declined to do so, as he wished to show himself in the town. He promised, however, to send his horse, and to come himself to dinner. This promise he kept, and having dined with Mrs. Stout and her daughter, he left the house about four o'clock, saying that he had business in the town, but that he would return in the evening. At nine he returned, asked for pen, ink, and paper to write to his wife, and had his supper. Mrs. Stout, the mother, went to bed, leaving Spencer Cowper and her daughter together, orders having been given to make a fire in his room. Between ten and eleven o'clock Sarah called the servant girl, and, in Cowper's hearing, desired her to warm his bed. She went up-stairs for that purpose, leaving Spencer Cowper and Sarah alone in the parlor together. As she went up-stairs she heard the house-clock (which was half an hour too fast) strike eleven. In about a quarter of an hour afterwards she heard the house-door shut to, and, supposing that Cowper had gone to post his letter, she remained warming his bed for a quarter of an hour longer. She then went down-stairs, and found that both Spencer Cowper and her young mistress were gone.

The mother could not be examined upon the trial, as she was a Quaker, and could not take an oath. The account of the transactions of that day, therefore, rests solely upon the evidence of Sarah Walker, the servant, who deponed as follows:

"May it please you, my lord, on Friday before the last assizes, Mr. Cowper's wife sent a letter to Mrs. Stout, that she might expect Mr. Cowper at the assize-time; and, therefore, we expected Mr. Cowper at that time, and accordingly provided; and as he came in with the judges, she asked him if he would alight? He said, 'No; by reason I came in later than usual, I will go into town and show myself,' but he would send his horse presently. She asked him how long it would be before he would come, because they would stay for him? He said he could not tell, but he would send her word; and she thought he had forgot, and sent me down to know whether he would please to come. He said he had business, and he could not come just then; but he came in less than a quarter of an hour after, and dined there, and he went away at four o'clock; and then my mistress asked him if he would lie there? And he answered yes, and he came at night about nine; and he sat talking about half an hour, and then called for pen, ink, and paper, for that, as he said, he was to write to his wife; which was brought him, and he wrote a letter; and then my mistress went and asked him what he would have for supper? He said milk, by reason he had made a good dinner; and I got him his supper, and he ate it; after, she called me in again, and they were talking together, and then she bid me make a fire in his chamber; and when I had done so, I came and told him of it, and he looked at me, and made me no answer; then she bid me warm the bed, which accordingly I went up to do as the clock struck eleven; and in about a quarter of an hour I heard the door shut, and I thought he was gone to convey the letter, and stayed about a quarter of an hour longer, and came down, and he was gone, and she; and Mrs. Stout, the mother, asked me the reason why he went out when I was warming his bed? And she asked me for my mistress, and I told her I left her with Mr. Cowper; and I never saw her after that, nor did Mr. Cowper return to the house." *

Cowper, who defended himself with great ability, asked the witness in cross-examination:

"When you came down and missed your mistress, did you inquire after her all that night?

"*A.*—No, sir, I did not go out of the doors; I thought you were with her, and so I thought she would come to no harm.

"*Mr. Cowper.*—Here is a whole night she gives no account of. Pray, mistress, why did you not go after her?

"*A.*—My mistress would not let me.

"*Mr. Cowper.*—Why would she not let you?

"*A.*—I said I would seek for her. 'No,' says she, 'by reason, if you go and seek for her, and do not find her, it will make an alarm over the town, and there may be no occasion.' " †

Maternal solicitude could not be very strong in the

* 13 State Trials, 1112. † Ibid, 1114.

breast of Mrs. Stout, or she was disposed to place a more than ordinary degree of confidence in the discretion of her daughter and young Cowper. Sarah Stout was never again seen alive. The next morning her body was found in a mill-dam something less than a mile distant. Cowper never returned to Mrs. Stout's; he was seen at an inn in the town at eleven, and arrived at other lodgings, which he had hired in the town, at a quarter past. Here the evidence ends. A vast amount of testimony was given at the trial, as to whether the body of the girl floated or not; as to whether a body thrown into the water after death would float or sink; but it came to nothing. The coroner's inquest had been hurried over, and no examination of the body had taken place until long after decomposition had proceeded too far to allow of any satisfactory result being arrived at.

In a former number* we observed on the effect of the rule of law which excludes a prisoner not only from giving evidence on his own behalf, but also from tendering himself for cross-examination. If Cowper was innocent, that rule bore hardly upon him in the present case. We will, however, give him the full benefit of his own account of the matter. He said †—and in this he was confirmed by the evidence of his brother—that having received a pressing invitation to take up his quarters during the assizes at Mrs. Stout's, he had resolved to do so, his object being to save the expense of other lodgings at the house of a person of the name of Barefoot, where

* *Ante*, Eliza Fenning's Case. † 13 State Trials, 1149.

he had been in the habit of staying with his brother. Finding that his brother would be detained in London by his parliamentary duties, he requested him to write and countermand the lodgings at Barefoot's. This he neglected to do, and on Spencer Cowper's arrival at Hertford he found them prepared for him. Finding that he should have at any rate to pay for these lodgings, which were nearer to the court-house and more commodious than Mrs. Stout's, he determined to occupy them. His account is as follows:

"My lord, as to my coming to this town on Monday, it was the first day of the assizes, and that was the reason that brought me hither; before I came out of town, I confess, I had a design to take a lodging at this gentlewoman's house, having been invited by letter so to do; and the reason why I did not was this: my brother, when he went the circuit, always favored me with the offer of a part of his lodgings, which, out of good husbandry, I always accepted. The last circuit was in Parliament-time, and my brother being in the money-chair, could not attend the circuit as he used to do; he had very good lodgings, I think one of the best in this town, where I used to be with him; these were always kept for him, unless notice was given to the contrary. The Friday before I came down to the assizes I happened to be in company with my brother and another gentleman, and then I showed them the letter by which I was earnestly invited down to lie at the house of this gentlewoman during the assizes [it is dated the 9th of March last]; and designing to comply with the invitation, I thereupon desired my brother to write to Mr. Barefoot, our landlord, and get him, if he could, to dispose of the lodgings; for, said I, if he keeps them, they must be paid for, and then I cannot well avoid lying there. My brother did say he would write, if he could think on it; and thus, if Mr. Barefoot disposed of the lodgings, I own I intended to lie at the deceased's house; but if not, I looked on myself obliged to lie at Mr. Barefoot's. Accordingly I shall prove, as soon as ever I came to this town, in the morning of the first day of the assizes, I went directly to Mr. Barefoot's, [the maid and all agreed in this] and the reason was, I had not seen my brother after he said he would write, before I went out to London; and therefore it was proper for me to go first to Mr. Barefoot's to know whether my brother had wrote to him, and whether he had disposed of his lodgings or not. As soon as I came to Mr. Barefoot's, I asked his wife and maid-servant, one after another, if they had received a letter from my brother to unbespeak the lodgings; they told me no, that the room was kept for us; and I think they had made a fire, and that the sheets were airing. I was a little concerned he had not writ; but being satisfied that no letter had been received, I said immediately, as I shall prove by several witnesses, if it be so, I must stay with you; I will take up my lodging here. Thereupon I alighted, and sent for my bag to the coffee-house, and lodged all my things at Barefoot's, and thus I took up my lodging there as usual. I had no sooner done this, but Sarah

Walker came to me from her mistress to invite me to dinner, and accordingly I went and dined there; and when I went away, it may be true, that, being asked, I said I would come again at night; but that I said I would lie there, I do positively deny; and knowing I could not lie there, it is unlikely I should say so. My lord, at night I did come again, and paid her some money that I received from Mr. Loftus, who is the mortgagor, for interest of the £200 I before mentioned [it was £6, odd money, in guineas and half-guineas]: I writ a receipt, but she declined the signing of it, pressing me to stay there that night; which I refused, as engaged to lie at Mr. Barefoot's, and took my leave of her; and that very money which I paid her was found in her pocket, as I have heard, after she was drowned." *

When Cowper recurs, at a later period of the trial, to the events of that night, he says: "Now, if your lordship pleases, I would explain that part of Sarah Walker the maid's evidence, when she says her mistress ordered her to warm the bed, and I never contradicted it." And after calling the attention of the court to the warm expressions contained in the letter he had received from the girl, he goes on:

"I had rather leave it to be observed than make the observation myself, what might be the dispute between us at the time the maid speaks of. I think it was not necessary she should be present at the debate; and therefore I might not interrupt her mistress or the orders she gave; but as soon as the

* 13 State Trials, 1150.

maid was gone I made use of these objections; and I told Mrs. Stout by what accident I was obliged to take up my lodging at Mr. Barefoot's, and that the family was sitting up for me; that my staying at her house under these circumstances would in all probability invoke the censure of the town and country, and that therefore I could not stay, whatever my inclination otherwise might be; but, my lord, my reasons not prevailing, I was forced to decide the controversy by going to my lodging; so that the maid may swear true when she says I did not contradict her orders." *

It will be observed that Cowper first puts his change of intention as to staying at Mrs. Stout's solely on the ground of having other lodgings on his hands. He says that until he found those lodgings were engaged, he had determined to take up his abode at Mrs. Stout's. The question was simply one of the cost of the lodgings. When, however, he has to account for the servant girl's evidence as to his consent to the preparations for his passing the night there, orders for which were given in his presence, then, for the first time, he begins to talk of "provoking the censure of the town and country." † It is impossible to know what took place after the servant girl left the room. Cowper himself leaves it unexplained whether he left Sarah Stout in the house, or whether she quitted it at the same time that he did. The latter would seem to be the more probable conjecture, from the fact that the door was only heard to shut once, and it was

* State Trials, 1170. † Ibid, 1177.

proved that it was not easy to shut the door without being heard. If Cowper had been entitled to submit himself to cross-examination, these facts might have been, and probably would have been, explained.

Here, not only the evidence, but the whole substance of Cowper's defense ends. The trial was prolonged by an enormous mass of testimony, partly from men of the highest eminence in the medical profession, and partly from persons who had seen great numbers of bodies, some of which had been thrown into the sea after death, and others of which had been drowned in naval engagements and shipwrecks, as to whether the fact of a body floating afforded any evidence that life was extinct before it had been thrown into the water. On this point the evidence was, as might be anticipated, contradictory, but had it been otherwise, it would have been of no value; for the question, whether Sarah Stout's body floated or sank, was not proved either one way or the other. It was found entangled among some stakes in the mill-dam, in a manner which rendered it impossible to say whether it was supported or kept down.* There

*See the evidence of Berry, Venables, Dell, Ulfe, Dew, Edmunds, Page, How, and Meager, 13 State Trials, 1116 to 1122. All these witnesses, who were present when the body was found in the mill-dam, agree in *asserting* that the body "floated," and they no doubt believed what they said, their evidence affording an example of how far a preconceived idea will affect belief; they describe the body as lying on the right side, the head and right arm being driven between the stakes, which were something less than a foot apart, by the stream. Robert Dew and Young, who were called on behalf of the prisoner, and who were also present when the body was taken out of the water, assert equally posi-

was, therefore, no basis on which to found the scientific evidence, and the case against Cowper rested upon a very few facts, and may be summed up in very few words. He was the last person in Sarah Stout's company. His conduct on leaving the house was mysterious and unexplained. When he left, instead of going direct to his lodgings, he went to the Glove and Dolphin Inn to pay a small bill for horse-keep. This had somewhat the appearance of a desire to secure evidence of an *alibi*. He was, on his own showing, embarrassed by Sarah Stout's pertinacious attachment, and had a stronger motive to get rid of her than has sometimes been found sufficient to prompt men to the most revolting crimes. On the other hand, it must be remembered that Cowper was not, like Tawell, a man who prided himself on his reputation for the respectabilities of life, but, as well as his more celebrated brother, a man of known libertinism, not likely to commit a crime of the deepest dye for the purpose of concealing a disreputable intrigue. To have convicted Cowper of murder upon this evidence would have

tively that the body *sank*—see p. 1151. These two witnesses describe the mode in which the body was entangled in the stakes with more particularity than the witnesses for the prosecution. The judge, in his charge to the jury, treated this evidence like a man of sense. "I shall not undertake," he said, "to give you the particulars of their evidence; but they tell you she lay on her right side, the one arm up even with the surface of the water, and her body under the water; but some of her clothes were above the water; particularly, one says, the ruffles of her left arm were above the water. You have heard, also, what the doctors and surgeons said, on the one side and the other, concerning the swimming and sinking of dead bodies in the water; *but I can find no certainty in it;* and I leave it to your consideration."—13 State Trials, 1188.

been, of course, impossible. But the case must ever remain shrouded in the darkest mystery. If not guilty of what the law defines as murder, there can be no doubt that Cowper's conduct was the immediate cause of the death of the unhappy girl. When the servant left the room they were on the most amicable terms. This is fixed by the evidence, as nearly as possible, at half-past ten by the town-clock. As the clock struck eleven, Cowper entered the Glove and Dolphin Inn.* In that short half-hour he had either incurred the guilt of murder, or by his unkindness had driven a woman, who loved him with the most devoted affection, to rush uncalled into the presence of her Maker. Cowper, if not a murderer, which we think he was not, must, at any rate, have been a man of a singularly cold and unfeeling disposition. According to his own version of the story, the girl, whom he had left only a few moments before, immediately upon his quitting her, sought a refuge from her love, her sorrows, and her shame, under the cold waters of the Priory river. On the next morning he heard of her fate, and the first thing he did was to send the hostler from the inn to her mother's house for his horse, fearing lest, if the coroner's jury should bring in a verdict of *felo de se*, the animal might, being found in her stable, be claimed as forfeited to the lord of the manor. From first to last there is not one word of tenderness or regret. He never went near the bereaved mother, but he attended the coroner's inquest, gave

* Evidence of Elizabeth Spurr, 13 State Trials, 1177.

his evidence with the utmost coolness, and the next day proceeded on circuit as if nothing unusual had taken place. Three other persons were indicted along with Cowper as the accomplices of his crime, but against them there was not even the shadow of a case. The jury, after deliberating for about half an hour, acquitted all the prisoners.

The relatives of Sarah Stout attempted to bring Cowper to a second trial by means of a proceeding now abolished, entitled "The Appeal of Murder." The attempt failed through the influence of the Cowpers, who tampered with the sheriff, and procured the destruction of the writs. The sheriff was fined and imprisoned for his misconduct, Holt, the Chief Justice, severely animadverting on the foul play which had been employed to impede the course of justice.* Cowper continued to practice at the bar, and was at last raised to the bench of the Court of Common Pleas, a remarkable instance of a man who had held up his hand on an arraignment for murder, trying others for the same offense. He is said to have learned a lesson of caution and mercy from his own experience, and to have been remarkable for both those qualities.

One might have supposed that poor Sarah Stout would have been allowed to sleep in peace, without having her name revived and her sad story made famous more than a century and a half after her death. But such was not to be her fate. The opportunity of a double fling at Quakers and Tories has been too great a temptation for Lord Macaulay. It

* Lord Raymond, i, 575, R. v. Toler—13 State Trials, 1199.

was a right-and-left shot at the game he loved best. Accordingly, in the fifth and concluding volume of his History, in that part which we are told by the editor he had left "fairly transcribed and revised," we find four pages devoted to the case of that unhappy girl. The whole passage is so eloquent, so picturesque, so ingenious in insinuation, so daring in the misrepresentation of facts and the distortion of evidence, and affords so good an epitome of the best and the worst qualities of the author, that we give it entire:

"One mournful tale, which called forth the strongest feelings of the contending factions, is still remembered as a curious part of the history of our jurisprudence, and especially of the history of our medical jurisprudence. No Whig member of the Lower House, with the single exception of Montague, filled a larger space in the public eye than William Cowper. In the art of conciliating an audience, Cowper was pre-eminent. His graceful and engaging eloquence cast a spell on juries; and the Commons, even in those stormy moments when no other defender of the administration could obtain a hearing, would always listen to him. He represented Hertford, a borough in which his family had considerable influence; but there was a strong Tory minority among the electors, and he had not won his seat without a hard fight, which had left behind it many bitter recollections. His younger brother, Spencer, a man of parts and learning, was fast rising into practice as a barrister on the home circuit.

"At Hertford resided an opulent Quaker family named Stout. A pretty young woman of this family had lately sunk into a melancholy, of a kind not very unusual in girls of strong sensibility and lively imagination, who are subject to the restraints of austere religious societies. Her dress, her looks, her gestures, indicated the disturbance of her mind. She sometimes hinted her dislike of the sect to which she belonged. She complained that a canting waterman, who was one of the brotherhood, had held forth against her at a meeting. She threatened to go beyond sea, to throw herself out of the window, to drown herself. To two or three of her associates she owned that she was in love; and on one occasion she plainly said that the man whom she loved was one whom she never could marry. In fact, the object of her fondness was Spencer Cowper, who was already married. She at length wrote to him in language which she never would have used if her intellect had not been disordered. He, like an honest man, took no advantage of her unhappy state of mind, and did his best to avoid her. His prudence mortified her to such a degree that on one occasion she went into fits. It was necessary, however, that he should see her when he came to Hertford at the spring assizes of 1699, for he had been intrusted with some money which was due to her on mortgage. He called on her for this purpose late one evening, and delivered a bag of gold to her. She pressed him to be the guest of her family, but he excused himself and retired. The next morning she was found dead among the stakes of a mill-dam on the stream called the Priory river. That she had destroyed herself there could be no reasonable doubt. The coroner's inquest found that she had drowned herself while in a state of mental derangement. But the family was unwilling to admit that she had shortened her own life, and looked about for somebody who might be accused of murdering her. The last person who could be proved to have been in her company was Spencer Cowper. It chanced that two attorneys and a scrivener, who had come down from town to the Hertford assizes, had been overheard, on that unhappy night, talking over their wine about the charms and flirtations of the handsome Quaker girl, in the light way in which such subjects are sometimes discussed even at the circuit tables and mess tables of our more refined generation. Some wild words, susceptible of a double meaning, were used about the way in which she had jilted one lover, and the way in which another lover would punish her for her coquetry. On no better grounds than these, her relations imagined that Spencer Cowper had, with the assistance of these three retainers of the law, strangled her, and thrown her corpse into the water. There was absolutely no evidence of the crime. There was no evidence that any one of the accused had any motive to commit such a crime; there was no evidence that Spencer Cowper had any connection with the persons who were said to be his accomplices. One of those persons, indeed, he had never seen. But no story is too absurd to be imposed on minds blinded by religious and political fanaticism.

"The Quakers and the Tories joined to raise a formidable clamor. The Quakers had, in those days, no scruples about capital punishments. They would, indeed, as Spencer Cowper said bitterly, but too truly, rather send four innocent men to the gallows than let it be believed that one who had their light within her had committed suicide. The Tories exulted in the prospect of winning two seats from the Whigs. The whole kingdom was divided between Stouts and Cowpers. At the summer assizes Hertford was crowded with anxious faces from London, and from parts of England more distant than London. The prosecution was conducted with a malignity and unfairness which to us seem almost incredible; and, unfortunately, the dullest and most ignorant judge of the twelve was on the bench. Cowper defended himself and those who were said to be his accomplices with admirable ability and self-possession. His brother, much more distressed than himself, sat near him through the long agony of that day. The case against the prisoners rested chiefly on the vulgar error that a human body found, as this girl's body had been found, floating in water, must have been thrown into the water while still alive. To prove this doctrine, the counsel for the Crown called medical practitioners, of whom nothing is now known except that some of them had been active against the Whigs at Hertford elections. To confirm the evidence of these gentlemen, two or three sailors were put into the witness-box. On the other side appeared an array of men of science whose names are still remembered. Among them was William Cowper—not a kinsman of the defendant, but the most celebrated anatomist that England had then produced. He was, indeed, the founder of a dynasty illustrious in the history of science; for he was the teacher of William Cheselden, and William Cheselden was the teacher of John Hunter. On the same side appeared Samuel Garth, who, among the physicians of the capital, had no rival except Radcliffe, and Hans Sloane, the founder of the magnificent museum which is one of the glories of our country. The attempt of the prosecutors to make the superstitions of the forecastle evidence, for the purpose of taking away the lives of men, was treated by these philosophers with just disdain. The stupid judge asked Garth what he could say in answer to the testimony of the seamen. 'My lord,' replied Garth, 'I say that they are mistaken. I will find seamen in abundance to swear that they have known whistling raise the wind.' The jury found the prisoners not guilty, and the report carried back to London by persons who had been present at the trial was, that everybody applauded the verdict, and that even the Stouts seemed to be convinced of their error. It is certain, however, that the malevolence of the defeated party soon revived in all its energy. The lives of the four men who had just been absolved were again attacked by means of the most absurd and odious proceeding known to our old law, the appeal of murder. This attack, too, failed. Every artifice of chicane was at length exhausted; and nothing was left to the disappointed sect and the disappointed faction except to calumniate those whom it had been found impossible to murder. In a succession of libels, Spencer Cowper was held up to the execration of the public. But the public did him justice. He rose to high eminence in his profession; he at length took his seat, with general applause, on the judicial bench, and there distinguished himself by the humanity which he never failed to show to unhappy men who stood, as he had stood, at the bar. Many who seldom trouble themselves about pedigrees may be interested by learning that he was the grandfather of that excellent man and excellent poet, William Cowper, whose writings have long been peculiarly loved and prized by the members of the religious community which, under a strong delusion, sought to slay his innocent progenitor.*

"Though Spencer Cowper had escaped with life and honor, the Tories had carried their point. They had secured against the next election the support of the Quakers of Hertford; and the consequence was, that the borough was lost to the family and to the party which had lately predominated there."

Notwithstanding the fact that Lord Macaulay has

*"It is curious that all Cowper's biographers with whom I am acquainted—Hayley, Southey, Grimshawe, Chalmers—mention the judge, the common ancestor of the poet, of his first love, Theodora Cowper, and of Lady Hesketh, but that none of these biographers makes the faintest allusion to the Hertford trial, the most remarkable event in the history of the family; nor do I believe that any allusion to that trial can be found in any of the poet's numerous letters."

given so large a space to this case, he has read it with more than ordinary carelessness. He says: "The case against the prisoner rested chiefly on the vulgar error that a human body found, as this poor girl's body had been found, floating in the water, must have been thrown into the water *while still alive*." * The argument was exactly the reverse. It was urged that the fact of her body floating proved that she was thrown into the water *after she was dead;* and it was sought to be inferred that she had been strangled—that if, as was argued on behalf of the prisoner, she had drowned herself, her body would have been filled with water, and would have sunk. The evidence as to whether the body did in fact float or sink, was, as we have seen, contradictory. The *post mortem* examination was delayed so long that the medical testimony had really no foundation of facts to rest upon. At the trial an attempt was made, on the part of the prisoner, to establish the insanity of the girl; but nothing more was proved than might be easily shown to have occurred in the case of any love-sick girl who was, or fancied herself, the victim of an unrequited passion. Lord Macaulay's treatment of this evidence is amusing. Three of the circumstances on which he relies to prove her insanity are: 1st, That "she sometimes hinted a dislike of the sect to which she belonged," which is rather an odd proof of insanity in the mouth of Lord Macaulay; 2d, That "she complained that a canting waterman, who was one of the brethren, had held forth against her at a meet-

* Vol. v, 238.

ing" (which happened to be true, and seems to be a tolerably reasonable ground of annoyance); and, 3d, That "to two or three of her associates she owned she was in love." (Alas for all young ladies from sixteen upwards, in white satin, and their confidantes in white linen, if this is to be taken as a proof of insanity!) But when Lord Macaulay comes to the facts connected with Cowper's writing to announce his intention of staying at the house, his dining there, his return in the evening, and his mysterous disappearance at night simultaneously with the girl, he condenses them into the following words: "He, *like an honest man*, took no advantage of her unhappy state of mind, and did his best to avoid her" (it was, to say the least, an odd mode of avoiding her that he adopted). "It was necessary, however, that he should see her when he came to Hertford at the spring assizes of 1699, for he had been intrusted with some money which was due to her on mortgage. He called on her, *for this purpose*, late one evening, and delivered a bag of gold to her." (The "bag" exists only in Lord Macaulay's imagination—the "gold" was the petty sum of six pounds and a few odd shillings, which Cowper had received for her as interest on a sum of £200 which he had placed out on mortgage on her behalf, and the payment of which certainly did not make it necessary that he should be with her from two till four, and again from nine till half-past ten at night.) "She pressed him," adds Lord Macaulay, "to be the guest of the family, but *he excused himself and retired*."

It is worth while, as a matter of philological curiosity, to enumerate over again the facts which one of the greatest masters of the English language can compress into the phrase—"he excused himself and retired." Cowper went to the house on his arrival in the town, dined there with the family, left at four, returned at nine, supped, wrote his letters, was present whilst his bed and his bedroom fire were ordered and the maid was sent up to warm his bed; sat alone until half-past ten o'clock at night with a girl who he knew was violently in love with him, who had been in the habit of addressing the most passionate letters to him under a feigned name, and then — "*abiit—excessit—evasit—erupit.*" His departure only announced by the slamming-to of the street-door. This is Lord's Macaulay's notion of "excusing himself and retiring." He and the girl disappeared together. In the morning he is at other lodgings in the town, and she a corpse in the mill-dam.

For the charge that Lord Macaulay makes that "the prosecution was conducted with a malignity and unfairness which to us seem almost incredible," we cannot discover the slightest ground. Certainly none is to be found in the very ample and detailed report in the "State Trials." Indeed, a far greater latitude was allowed to the prisoner in his defense than would be permitted at the present day. What authority Lord Macaulay may have had for describing Hatsell, who presided at the trial, as "the dullest and most ignorant judge of the twelve," we know not. He seems to have tried the case with strict impartiality and very fair ability, and his charge to the jury was decidedly in favor of the prisoners.

We have frequently had occasion to remark upon the caution which ought to be observed before relying upon Lord Macaulay's marks of quotation. An amusing instance of this occurs in the passage we have just cited. A sailor of the name of Clement deponed that he had frequently observed that when a corpse was thrown into the sea it floated; whereas, if a man fell into the water and was drowned, his body sank as soon as life was extinct. In confirmation of this, he cited his own experience at the fight off Beachy Head, where the bodies of the men who were killed floated about; and at a shipwreck, where between five and six hundred men were drowned, whose bodies sank. This evidence was curious, and if it had been proved whether Sarah Stout's body floated or sank, would have been valuable. The judge felt, no doubt, that it was so; and when Garth swore that "it was *impossible* the body should have floated," and boldly stated his belief that "*all* dead bodies fall to the bottom unless they be prevented by some extraordinary tumor,"* he directed his attention to the evidence which had been given, and asked him "what he said as to the sinking of dead bodies in water?" Garth replied that, "if a strangled body be thrown into the water, the lungs being filled with air, and a cord left about the neck, it was possible it might float, because of

* 13 State Trials, 1157.

the included air, as a bladder would." Upon this the judge called his attention to the question as follows:

"*Baron Hatsell.*—But you do not observe my question: the seamen said that those that die at sea and are thrown overboard, if you do not tie a weight to them, they will not sink—what do you say to that?

"*Dr. Garth.*—My lord, no doubt in this thing they are mistaken. The seamen are a superstitious people: they fancy that whistling at sea will occasion a tempest. *I must confess I have never seen anybody thrown overboard;* but I have tried some experiments on other dead animals, and they will certainly sink; we have tried them since we came hither." *

Now in this, we confess, it seems to us that the judge appears to greater advantage than the physician. Garth was evidently desirous to evade the question, and he attempted to do so by a sneer. The superstition of the sailors had nothing to do with the question whether a man killed in battle and falling into the water floats or sinks. Garth was compelled to admit that he had no experience on the subject. He said, and said truly, that "the object of tying weights to a body is to prevent it from floating at all, which otherwise would happen in some few days." † The well-known instance of the floating of the body of Caracciolo, notwithstanding the weights which were attached to his feet,

* State Trials, 1158. † Ibid.

will occur at once to the mind of the reader. The inquiry of the judge was pertinent to the evidence, and the reply might have been material to the question of the guilt or innocence of the prisoner. Lord Macaulay disposes of both question and answer in the following words: "The *stupid* judge asked Garth what he could say in answer to the testimony of the seamen. 'My lord,' replied Garth, 'I say that they are mistaken. I will find seamen in abundance to swear that they have known whistling raise the wind.'" There was no stupidity that we can discover in the question, and the answer is misquoted.

Lord Macaulay, however, does not trouble himself with the facts of the case. He finds for once the Quakers and the Tories united, (or rather, we ought to say, he assumes their union; for from first to last in the trial there is not a particle of evidence that political feeling intervened) and he infers that they could only be united for the purpose of committing a judicial murder; that the object of the Quakers was to "send four innocent men to the gallows rather than let it be believed that one who had their light within her had committed suicide,"* and that the Tories were urged on to the same atrocity by "the prospect of winning two seats from the Whigs." Lord Macaulay makes no account of the feelings that would be awakened amongst relations, friends, and neighbors, by the sudden and violent death of a young and beautiful girl, who, whether murdered or not, had unques-

* Vol. v, 237.

tionably been cruelly trifled with by a man who, if not directly, was at any rate indirectly the cause of her death. "Religious and political fanaticism" are motives the power of which Lord Macaulay was certainly not likely to underrate. Yet it might have been supposed that the religion of Sarah Stout was one which he would have been disposed to treat, if not with respect, at least with tenderness, however mistaken his more mature convictions might lead him to consider it to be.

We have ourselves little sympathy with the peculiar tenets and habits of the Quakers. It is difficult for any one to write with perfect justice about that very singular sect. A body of Christians who make it part of their religion to observe the strictest rules of grammar in the use of the singular and plural of the personal pronouns, whilst they habitually violate them as to the nominative and accusative; whose consciences are tender as to buttons; who hold gay colors to be "unfriendly," whilst they delight in the richest and most costly fabrics; who shrink from the hypocrisy of addressing a stranger as "Dear Sir," while they have no scruple in calling the man they most despise "Respected Friend," merely commit amusing eccentricities. The evil is much more serious when they proscribe all those arts which tend most to brighten our course through life. Literature, except of the most dreary kind, is prohibited to strict Friends. We once made a passing allusion to Mr. Jonathan Oldbuck, in conversation with one of the most eminent Quakers of the day, a member of a learned profession, and discovered, to our astonishment, that he was in total ignorance of the "Waverly Novels." Another venerable and strict Friend, seeing a volume lettered "Horatii Opera" on the table of one of his laxer brethren, shook his head gravely, and said, "Thou knowest, friend, that we have a testimony against all operas." Nothing can be conceived more desolate than a pure Quaker library: Barclay's "Apology" and Baxter's "Saint's Rest," Penn's "No Cross, no Crown," and George Fox's "Journal"—perhaps, by extraordinary good fortune, "Paradise Lost" and "The Task"—all excellent in their way, but not exactly the books to while away a tedious hour; and one looks in vain for Shakespeare and Scott, for Pope or Fielding. Painting and music share the same fate. Now and then, however, happily, the old Adam is too strong, and such arts are cultivated either "clandecently," as Mawworm says, or in open defiance of the yearly meeting. Gastronomy is the only one of the liberal arts that flourishes unrestrained. The Quakers are a hospitable people; their dinners are excellent and their wines super-excellent. The whitest linen, the most brilliant silver, and the most sparkling glass, are to be found at their tables. They indulge, not to excess, but silently and thankfully, in these good things, and a certain serious rotundity has in consequence become hereditary amongst them. The late Lord Macaulay himself inherited something of this formation, modified, however, by the admixture which his blood had received from the lean and hungry Celts to whom he owed his Highland name.

This formation is no doubt unfavorable to great personal activity; but personal activity is of little import to a Quaker. Field sports, and their attendant festivities of all kinds, are prohibited. A Quaker thinks of a hunt-ball as if it were a war dance of wild Indians. But here, again, nature will sometimes assert her rights. We have known a Quaker to be an excellent judge of a horse, and some of the best heavy weights across the Pytchly and Warwickshire countries have been of pure Quaker blood. We once heard of a Quaker horse-dealer. But of all strange sights, a Quaker child is the strangest. To find a little curly-headed darling of four or five years old, who, instead of climbing on one's knee, and insisting vociferously on a game at romps or a fairy story before it will go to bed, walks off demurely with a "Fare thee well, friend," is enough to make one's hair stand on end.

Early as this discipline begins, it is pleasant to find that nature is sometimes too strong for it. We have lately met with a narrative (published within the last six months) of a Quaker journey in America, writ by one William Tallack, a Friend, who, if we are to judge of him by his book, must be dry enough to satisfy the most nervous dread of any approach to that humidity which constitutes a "wet Quaker"—a being peculiarly abhorrent to consistent Friends. After devoting many pages to bonnets with round crowns, and bonnets with square crowns, buttons and straps, knee shorts, and "slit collars," and those still more execrable abominations, "turned-down collars with slits in them" (though, we confess, without making it by any means clear to one of the profane what constitutes a slit collar); after recording how one Elias Hicks "felt that his conscience required the relinquishment of unnecessary buttons to his coat," and compelled him to "turn up a cushion in the meeting, and to seat himself on the hard board,"* he gives some extracts from the records of the Quakers' meeting, amongst which it is really refreshing to meet the passions and the foibles of poor human nature.

Here is the confession of a warm-tempered Friend, who probably would have been all the better for the cooling discipline he administered to his neighbor, even at the risk of the dreaded consequence of becoming "wet."

"Whereas, I contended with my neighbor, W. S., for what I apprehended to be my right, by endeavoring to turn a certain stream of water into its natural course, till it rose to a personal difference, in which dispute I gave way to warmth of temper so far as to *put my friend W. into the pond;* for which action of mine, being contrary to the good order of Friends, I am sorry, and desire, through divine assistance, to live in unity with him for the future." †

*It is to be hoped that Elias Hicks never became subject to the inconvenient delusion recorded by Melander of an unhappy man, "qui opinatus est, ex vitro sibi constatas clunes, sic ut omnia sua negotia atque actiones stando perficeret, metuens, ne, si in sedile se inclinaret, natefrangeret, ac vitri fragmenta hinc inde dissilirent."—Melan., *Joco-Seria*, 433.

† Friendly Sketches in America, by William Tallack.

But it is not to wrath alone that Friends sometimes give way. A gentler passion occasionally hurries them beyond the bounds of what is strictly "friendly."

"Whereas, I was too forward and hasty in making suit to a young woman after the death of my wife, having made some proceedings that way in less than four months, which I am now sensible was wrong. As witness my hand, R. H." *

Even that peaceful union which we are bound to suppose a Quaker marriage to be (by the way, what a very odd proceeding a Quaker courtship must be! how do they get married at all?) is sometimes disturbed by the sinful passions of humanity. Thus we find that the "Concord preparation-meeting complains of J. P. S. for breach of his marriage covenants in refusing to live with his wife, as a faithful husband ought to do."

Nor does the traveler fail to observe the hospitality which we have already noticed as so commendable amongst Friends, but which is sometimes carried to an inconvenient excess.

"At meals," he says, "there is generally several times the quantity of food placed upon the table which could possibly be eaten by the heartiest appetites of those present, and plates are piled with so much that they are seldom empty at the end of the meal. * * It is usual to help a visitor to two or three slices of pie at a time."

*Friendly Sketches in America, 195.

Times have certainly changed amongst the Quakers since

> "Brother Green was feasted
> With a spiritual collation
> By our frugal mayor,
> Who can dine with a prayer,
> And sup with an exhortation."

Still it must be admitted by all candid men that Quakerism has its estimable as well as its ridiculous side, and that a sect which can number amongst its followers such men as William Penn, Elwood, the friend of Milton, Barclay, Clarkson, Reynolds, the philanthropist, and Dalton, the philosopher, deserves a treatment far different from that which it has received from Lord Macaulay. To assert, without one particle of evidence to support the statement, that the Quakers deliberately planned a judicial murder to conceal the fact that one of their body had committed suicide, is just as monstrous as to impute to the Tories that they were accomplices in the crime. This unscrupulous treatment of facts, and equally unscrupulous suggestion of motives, is one of the most dangerous weapons a combatant can wield. No instrument of attack is so easily turned against the party making use of it. If a historian could be found equally unscrupulous as Lord Macaulay, and as deeply imbued with opposite prejudices, nothing would be easier than to paraphrase his account of Spencer Cowper's trial almost in his own words, and with far less departure from the facts. The narrative would then assume something of the following form: "At Hertford resided a respectable Quaker family named Stout. One daughter, a beautiful girl of strong sensibility and lively imagination, formed a deep attachment to Spencer Cowper. He trifled with her affections, took every advantage of her unhappy state of mind, and then cast her off and married another woman. Her almost frantic attachment still continued. She wrote letters to him breathing the deepest passion. He paraded them before his brother (who was a man of notoriously loose habits) and his other profligate associates. When he came to the Hertford spring assizes in 1699, he went direct to her mother's house. He dined and supped there; he spent the evening in affectionate conversation with the girl he had betrayed. His bed was prepared in the house, and the servant-girl was sent up to warm it. Spencer Cowper and Sarah Stout were left together in the parlor—from that moment she was never seen alive. They left the house together at half-past ten at night, and in the morning her corpse was discovered in the mill-dam. It would perhaps be going too far to assert that Cowper was certainly her murderer, but the case was one of the darkest suspicion. He was placed upon his trial for murder, but to anticipate a conviction would have been absurd. The law closed the mouth of the principal witness, the mother of the girl, for she was a Quaker, and could not take an oath. The judge, a friend of the Cowpers, indulged the prisoner in a degree of license in his defense which in the present day would not be tolerated. The Cowpers were powerful in Hertford, which was represented in Parliament by the father and the brother of the prisoner. Every artifice that could influence the minds of the jury against Quakers and Tories was resorted to. Every prejudice of religious or political fanaticism against an unpopular sect and an obnoxious party was appealed to. The consequence was that Cowper was acquitted. An attempt was made to place him on his trial a second time by means of an 'appeal of murder,' a proceeding which Lord Holt, in this very case, designated as 'a noble badge of the liberties of an Englishman.' But here again the influence of the powerful family of the Cowpers paralyzed the arm of justice. The sheriff was tampered with and the writ destroyed. The sheriff paid the penalty of his misconduct by imprisonment and fine, and was subjected to a severe rebuke from Lord Holt. The Cowpers triumphed, but their exultation was short. Outraged humanity vindicated its rights. The press teemed with indignant pamplets, and at the next election both the Cowpers were ignominiously ejected from the representation of their native town." *

Such is the mode in which this subject may be treated, when, as in the old fable, the lion turns sculptor. It is far nearer the truth than Lord Macaulay's own. To gratify his political and family aversions, Lord Macaulay has raked up the

*"It is hardly necessary to remind any student of English history that Spencer Cowper and Sarah Stout are the Mosco and Zara of 'The New Atlantis.' See Vol. i, 166, 174, for a very full account of this unhappy transaction. Lord Macaulay, who has drawn largely upon the stores of this work in other instances, appears to have overlooked the fact that this narrative was to be found in the pages of a contemporary historian, whose character for accuracy is second only to his own."

ashes of poor Sarah Stout, and has revived a very discreditable incident in the history of a very eminent family. He expresses surprise that none of the biographers of the poet Cowper should have alluded to this adventure of his grandfather. An old proverb might have told him that there are certain families amongst whom it is a breach of good manners to make any mention of "hemp." We think it was Quin who once introduced Foote to a company as "a gentleman whose father was hanged for murdering his uncle." Polite and pious biographers, such as Hayley and Southey, generally avoid all allusion to such disagreeable subjects. Lord Macaulay is puzzled by what appears to him unnecessary delicacy, and has made the whole scandalous story (for scandalous it must remain, even taking the most favorable view) as notorious as possible. Where one reader dives into the "State Trials," a thousand will read Lord Macaulay's fifth volume; and all the world now has the advantage of knowing that the grandfather of "that excellent man, and excellent poet," as Lord Macaulay justly calls William Cowper, behaved extremely ill to a pretty Quaker girl, and had a narrow escape from being hanged for murdering her.

INDEX.

A.

B.

C.

D.

E.

F.

G.

H.

I.

J.

K.

L.

M.

N.

O.

P.

Q.

R.

S.

T.

U.

V.

W.

www.ingramcontent.com/pod-product-compliance
Lightning Source LLC
LaVergne TN
LVHW021407110826
845150LV00007B/1824

9781425511784